"John 3:16 is the North Star of the Bible. If you align your life with it, you can find The Way home."

-Anne Graham Lotz, AnGel Ministries

"I remember vividly that I walked down an aisle in a church one night, without prompting by my parents, and knelt at a humble altar. There through my tears, I gave my heart to Jesus. I was three years old. That night proved to be the highlight of my entire life. The "whosoever" in John 3:16 even extended to a little toddler. Praise the Lord!"

-Dr. James Dobson, Founder of Focus on the Family

"To me, John 3:16 is the very foundation of my faith. It is because of God's love that He gave and it's because of God's love that I am saved forever."

-CeCe Winans, Gospel Music Artist

"There it is in black and white. As simple and gentle as 1+1=2. For God so loved the world that He gave His only son and whoever believes in Him shall NOT perish, but shall have everlasting life. That's it. Admission is free."

-Delilah, Radio Host

"This is the first verse that I learned as a child and it changed my life. To most 10 year olds, these would be sweet words to recite to Mom and Dad to make them smile. To me they were a lighthouse in the darkness, a concrete promise when everything else seemed untrue and a hope that could not be extinguished. Over forty years later I wrap the truth of these words around me everyday as I look for others who are lost at sea, betrayed and hopeless. All the literature in the world cannot compete with the treasure contained in these twenty-six words."

-Sheila Walsh, Author of *God Has a Dream for Your Life*

"We can *all* endure a great deal of pain and grief, and general "life-is-not-fair" experiences when we know who *loves* us, and how incredible and incomprehensible the *joy* is that awaits us."

-Michael Blanton, Artist Management

"Out of great need is born great faith. I have seen both. 3:16 brings life and faith to a hope-starved world. May we embrace its message anew."

-Bishop John K. Rucyahana, Anglican Bishop of Shyira Diocese
in Rwanda and Author of *The Bishop of Rwanda*

"John 3:16 is the foundation of my faith. A picture of undeserved, unconditional, and unwavering love from a Father to his kids."

-Ernie Johnson, Sportscaster-TNT/TBS

"When I was a boy I used to hug a rubber hot water bottle in bed at night to beat off the chill air from the frigid Irish Sea. Comfort! I woke up wet, cold, and miserable. The rubber hot water bottle had perished. It had slowly deteriorated, imperceptibly disintegrated and was ultimately useless. Perished! That can happen to humans too—and God so loved the world that He gave us Jesus so that we would not perish but have everlasting life."

-Stuart Briscoe, Author of *What Works When Life Doesn't*

"I love John 3:16 because it is the gospel in a nutshell. It shares God's great love for us, and our great need for him."

-Mac Powell, Lead Singer of Third Day

"There are hundreds of verses in scripture that are of significant importance to me. But this is the most important verse in the Bible."

-John Smoltz, Atlanta Braves Pitcher

"This is the promise that bears hope for the hopeless. When we finally realize "I can't do this on my own" this is the Father responding, "I know, so I've done it for you."

-Jeff Foxworthy, Comedian

"John 3:16 is the Mount Everest of Scripture passages from God's Word. In this great verse, we see the highest statement of Theology as it portrays God's nature as a God who deeply loves. It portrays the genius of Soteriology as it shows how God planned to rescue mankind through the gift of His Son, Jesus. John 3:16 sums up God's nature, God's plan, and God's intent."

-Frank S. Page, President of The Southern Baptist Convention

"By twenty I was visibly unraveling mentally and emotionally. It would take the harrowing experience of living as an agoraphobic before I considered God's intervening love and relinquished my heart to Christ. 3:16 is the undeniable address my sanity, safety, and eternal security takes refuge in."

-Patsy Clairmont, Author of *Dancing Bones*

"God's love is not some mere sentiment, but rather something that He showed in a tangible way. God offers to us the gift of eternal life. To receive a gift, you must reach out to accept it, and then open it."

-Greg Laurie, Pastor/Evangelist

"John 3:16. What an amazing scripture—God loved us while we were quite unlovable people. He reached out to us when we were unreachable. Knowing that we would fail Him, deny Him, and spurn this unconditional love, He still gave...unconditionally!"

-Don Moen, Singer/Songwriter

"God gave his son as payment for our sins, everyone's sins—the payment was as horrible as anything you can imagine. Beyond the physical pain, the experience of separation from his Father was a pain that cannot be described. But Jesus endured this for us so that we can enjoy eternal life."

-Ned Yost, Manager of the Milwaukee Brewers

"Without hope, the fear of death is overwhelming. But as Christians, the Bible verse John 3:16 assures us that there is everlasting life—and this promise alone should give all of us hope at the time of death."

-Kenneth Cooper, M.D., M.P.H.

Reflections on 3:16 the book

"Lucado digs deeply into one of the most famous and oft-quoted passages of the Bible—John 3:16. First situating it in its biblical context as part of Jesus' conversation with Nicodemus, Lucado then dissects the 26-word promise phrase by phrase, picking out key theological ideas that provide hope to Christians. What does it mean that God 'so loved the world?' What must we do to gain everlasting life? Using his trademark folksy style, Lucado employs great stories and real-life illustrations to drive home points about God's love, justice and determination to save."

-*Publishers Weekly*

"Max gave us humor and charm in *Hermie and Wormie*. Now he has given us faith and wisdom."

-Tim Conway, Actor

"My friend Max Lucado has done it again! He's taken the most beloved passage of Scripture, unwrapped its deepest truths revealing the greatest expression of God's love. *3:16*'s message of hope will show you how much you matter to God. This is a must read for anyone."

-Rick Warren, Pastor of Saddleback Church
and Author of *The Purpose Driven Life*

"I'm a sucker for a simple love story. Want to learn why on earth you are on this earth? Want to learn how to really love? Read this book. Max has taken the single most important (and simple) verse in the Bible and dissected it for those of us who need to keep it simple."

-Rick Perry, Governor of Texas

"At the heart of our worship is the message of John 3:16. The story still inspires—out of God's great love was born great sacrifice. In *3:16*, Max makes new and fresh one of the oldest and deepest truths of our faith. I cannot help but sing and shout and dance from a grateful and humble heart when I think of what God has done for me and all of humanity. How great is our God!"

-Chris Tomlin, Singer/Songwriter

"Whether you are kicking the tires of Christianity or you cut your teeth on a church pew, *3:16* promises to broaden your horizons and further your understanding of God's most fundamental, life-transforming promise—the promise of eternal life."

-Ed Young, Pastor of Fellowship Church and
Author of *Outrageous, Contagious Joy*

"Max Lucado brings words, and now numbers, to new life. The truth in 3:16 is life changing, and nobody makes it more relevant for today and compelling for the future than our friend Max."

-Mary Graham, President of Women of Faith

"One of America's favorite authors helps us to see this precious gem from a variety of perspectives, each of which sheds additional light on an inexhaustible truth."

-Tony Campolo, Ph. D., Professor of Sociology at Eastern University

3:16

ALSO BY MAX LUCADO

Published in Nashville, Tennessee, by Thomas Nelson. Thomas Nelson is a trademark of Thomas Nelson, Inc.

Thomas Nelson, Inc. books may be purchased in bulk for educational, business, fund-raising, or sales promotional use. For information, please e-mail SpecialMarkets@ThomasNelson.com.

Library of Congress Cataloging-in-Publication Data

Lucado, Max.
  3:16 / Max Lucado.
    p. cm.
  Includes bibliographical references.
  ISBN 10: 0-8499-0193-6 (hardcover)
  ISBN 13: 978-0-8499-0193-5 (hardcover)
  ISBN-10: 0-8499-1981-9 (IE)
  ISBN-13: 978-0-8499-1981-7 (IE)

  1. Bible. N.T. John III, 16--Criticism, interpretation, etc. 2. Salvation--Christianity I. Title. II. Title: Three sixteen.
  BS2615.6.S25L83 2007
  226.5'06--dc22

                                                                      2007015849

With pride as deep and powerful as the Gulf Stream,
Denalyn and I dedicate this book
to our daughter Sara on her eighteenth birthday.
If you receive half the joy you've given us,
you'll radiate the rest of your life.
We love you.

CONTENTS

CONTENTS

ACKNOWLEDGMENTS

May I thank some people who helped this book become one?

Liz Heaney and Karen Hill were, as always, apt editors: equally skilled with surgical blades and soothing balm.

Steve and Cheryl Green tirelessly pastored these ideas and oversaw the hectic process of publication.

Carol "Bloodhound" Bartley let no slipup slip by uncorrected.

Susan and Greg Ligon and the entire Thomas Nelson team were the Fort Knox of creativity.

Dave Drury contributed dozens of helpful insights and suggestions.

David Treat offered hours of heaven-heeded intercessions.

The UpWords team makes all our lives easier.

The Oak Hills Church has, for two decades, tolerated my teachings and forgiven my shortcomings. I'm grateful to each of you.

Jenna, Andrea, and Sara. What dad deserves such splendid daughters? (Return to the nest anytime you like.)

Denalyn, I'm confused. I thought our honeymoon was supposed

to last ten days. My, it's been twenty-five years, and we're still celebrating! Did you book this trip?

And one final prayer to the Giver of all words. Eternal thanks, dear King. Would you convince the ones who read these words that the best of life is yet to be?

1

THE MOST FAMOUS CONVERSATION IN THE BIBLE

He's waiting for the shadows. Darkness will afford the cover he covets. So he waits for the safety of nightfall. He sits near the second-floor window of his house, sipping olive-leaf tea, watching the sunset, biding his time. Jerusalem enchants at this hour. The disappearing sunlight tints the stone streets, gilds the white houses, and highlights the blockish temple.

Nicodemus looks across the slate roofs at the massive square: gleaming and resplendent. He walked its courtyard this morning. He'll do so again tomorrow. He'll gather with religious leaders and do what religious leaders do: discuss God. Discuss reaching God, pleasing God, appeasing God.

God.

Pharisees converse about God. And Nicodemus sits among them. Debating. Pondering. Solving puzzles. Resolving dilemmas. *Sandal-tying on the Sabbath. Feeding people who won't work. Divorcing your wife. Dishonoring parents.*

What does God say? Nicodemus needs to know. It's his job. He's a holy man and leads holy men. His name appears on the elite list of Torah scholars. He dedicated his life to the law and occupies one of the seventy-one seats of the Judean supreme court. He has credentials, clout, and questions.

Questions for this Galilean crowd-stopper. This backwater teacher who lacks diplomas yet attracts people. Who has ample time for the happy-hour crowd but little time for clergy and the holy upper crust. He banishes demons, some say; forgives sin, others claim; purifies temples, Nicodemus has no doubt. He witnessed Jesus purge Solomon's Porch.[1] He saw the fury. Braided whip, flying doves. "There will be no pocket padding in my house!" Jesus erupted. By the time the dust settled and coins landed, hustling clerics were running a background check on him. The man from Nazareth won no favor in the temple that day.

So Nicodemus comes at night. His colleagues can't know of the meeting. They wouldn't understand. But Nicodemus can't wait until they do. As the shadows darken the city, he steps out, slips unseen through the cobbled, winding streets. He passes servants lighting lamps in the courtyards and takes a path that ends at the door of a simple house. Jesus and his followers are staying here, he's been told. Nicodemus knocks.

The noisy room silences as he enters. The men are wharf workers and tax collectors, unaccustomed to the highbrow world of a scholar. They shift in their seats. Jesus motions for the guest to sit. Nicodemus does and initiates the most famous conversation in the Bible: "Rabbi, we know that You are a teacher come from God; for no one can do these signs that You do unless God is with him" (John 3:2 NKJV).

Nicodemus begins with what he "knows." *I've done my home-work,* he implies. *Your work impresses me.*

We listen for a kindred salutation from Jesus: "And I've heard of you, Nicodemus." We expect, and Nicodemus expected, some hospitable chitchat.

None comes. Jesus makes no mention of Nicodemus's VIP status, good intentions, or academic credentials, not because they don't exist, but because, in Jesus's algorithm, they don't matter. He simply issues this proclamation: "Unless one is born again, he cannot see the kingdom of God" (v. 3 NKJV).

Behold the Continental Divide of Scripture, the international date line of faith. Nicodemus stands on one side, Jesus on the other, and Christ pulls no punches about their differences.

Nicodemus inhabits a land of good efforts, sincere gestures, and hard work. Give God your best, his philosophy says, and God does the rest.

Jesus's response? Your best won't do. Your works don't work. Your finest efforts don't mean squat. Unless you are born again, you can't even see what God is up to.

Nicodemus hesitates on behalf of us all. Born again? "How can a man be born when he is old?" (v. 4 NKJV). You must be kidding. Put life in reverse? Rewind the tape? Start all over? We can't be born again.

Oh, but wouldn't we like to? A do-over. A try-again. A reload. Broken hearts and missed opportunities bob in our wake. A mulligan would be nice. Who wouldn't cherish a second shot? But who can pull it off? Nicodemus scratches his chin and chuckles. "Yeah, a graybeard like me gets a maternity-ward recall."

Jesus doesn't crack a smile. "Most assuredly, I say to you, unless one is born of water and the Spirit, he cannot enter the kingdom of God" (v. 5 NKJV). About this time a gust of wind blows a few leaves through the still-open door. Jesus picks one off the floor and holds it up. God's power works like that wind, Jesus explains. Newborn hearts are born of heaven. You can't wish, earn, or create one. New birth? Inconceivable. God handles the task, start to finish.

Nicodemus looks around the room at the followers. Their blank expressions betray equal bewilderment.

Old Nick has no hook upon which to hang such thoughts. He speaks self-fix. But Jesus speaks—indeed introduces—a different language. Not works born of men and women, but a work done by God.

Born again. Birth, by definition, is a passive act. The enwombed child contributes nothing to the delivery. Postpartum celebrations applaud the work of the mother. No one lionizes the infant. ("Great work there, little one.") No, give the tyke a pacifier not a medal. Mom deserves the gold. She exerts the effort. She pushes, agonizes, and delivers.

When my niece bore her first child, she invited her brother and mother to stand in the delivery room. After witnessing three hours of pushing, when the baby finally crowned, my nephew turned to his mom and said, "I'm sorry for every time I talked back to you."

The mother pays the price of birth. She doesn't enlist the child's assistance or solicit his or her advice. Why would she? The baby can't even take a breath without umbilical help, much less navigate a path into new life. Nor, Jesus is saying, can we. Spiritual rebirthing requires a capable parent, not an able infant.

Who is this parent? Check the strategically selected word *again*. The Greek language offers two choices for *again*:[2]

1. *Palin,* which means a repetition of an act; to redo what was done earlier.[3]
2. *Anothen,* which also depicts a repeated action, but requires the original source to repeat it. It means "from above, from a higher place, things which come from heaven or God."[4] In other words, the one who did the work the first time does it again. This is the word Jesus chose.

The difference between the two terms is the difference between a painting by da Vinci and one by me. Suppose you and I are standing in the Louvre, admiring the famous *Mona Lisa.* Inspired by the work, I produce an easel and canvas and announce, "I'm going to paint this beautiful portrait again."

And I do! Right there in the Salle des Etats, I brandish my palette and flurry my brush and re-create the *Mona Lisa.* Alas, Lucado is no Leonardo. Ms. Lisa has a Picassoesque imbalance to her—crooked nose and one eye higher than the other. Technically, however, I keep my pledge and paint the *Mona Lisa again.*

Jesus means something else. He employs the second Greek term, calling for the action of the original source. He uses the word *anothen,* which, if honored in the Paris gallery, would require da Vinci's presence. *Anothen* excludes:

Latter-day replicas.

Second-generation attempts.

Well-meaning imitations.

He who did it first must do it again. The original creator recreates his creation. This is the act that Jesus describes.

Born: God exerts the effort.

Again: God restores the beauty.

We don't *try* again. We need, not the muscle of self, but a miracle of God.

The thought coldcocks Nicodemus. "How can this be?" (v. 9). Jesus answers by leading him to the Hope diamond of the Bible.

> For God
> so loved the world
> that he gave his one and only Son,
> that whoever believes in him
> shall not perish but have
> eternal life.

A twenty-six-word parade of hope: beginning with God, ending with life, and urging us to do the same. Brief enough to write on a napkin or memorize in a moment, yet solid enough to weather two thousand years of storms and questions. If you know nothing of the Bible, start here. If you know everything in the Bible, return here. We all need the reminder. The heart of the human problem is the heart of the human. And God's treatment is prescribed in John 3:16.

He loves.

He gave.

We believe.

We live.

The words are to Scripture what the Mississippi River is to America—an entryway into the heartland. Believe or dismiss them, embrace or reject them, any serious consideration of Christ must include them. Would a British historian dismiss the Magna Carta? Egyptologists overlook the Rosetta stone? Could you ponder the words of Christ and never immerse yourself into John 3:16?

The verse is an alphabet of grace, a table of contents to the Christian hope, each word a safe-deposit box of jewels. Read it again, slowly and aloud, and note the word that snatches your attention. "For God so loved the world that he gave his one and only Son, that whoever believes in him shall not perish but have eternal life."

"God so *loved* the world . . ." We'd expect an anger-fueled God. One who punishes the world, recycles the world, forsakes the world . . . but loves the world?

The *world*? This world? Heartbreakers, hope-snatchers, and dream-dousers prowl this orb. Dictators rage. Abusers inflict. Reverends think they deserve the title. But God loves. And he loves the world so much he gave his:

Declarations?

Rules?

Dicta?

Edicts?

No. The heart-stilling, mind-bending, deal-making-or-breaking claim of John 3:16 is this: *God gave his son . . . his only son.* No abstract ideas but a flesh-wrapped divinity. Scripture equates Jesus with God. God, then, gave himself. Why? So that "*whoever* believes in him shall not perish."

John Newton, who set faith to music in "Amazing Grace," loved this barrier-breaking pronoun. He said, "If I read 'God so loved the world, that He gave His only begotten Son, that when John Newton believed he should have everlasting life,' I should say, perhaps, there is some other John Newton; but 'whosoever' means this John Newton and the other John Newton, and everybody else, whatever his name may be."[5]

Whoever . . . a universal word.

9

And *perish* . . . a sobering word. We'd like to dilute, if not delete, the term. Not Jesus. He pounds Do Not Enter signs on every square inch of Satan's gate and tells those hell-bent on entering to do so over his dead body. Even so, some souls insist.

In the end, some perish and some live. And what determines the difference? Not works or talents, pedigrees or possessions. Nicodemus had these in hoards. The difference is determined by our belief. "Whoever *believes* in him shall not perish but have eternal life."

Bible translators in the New Hebrides islands struggled to find an appropriate verb for *believe*. This was a serious problem, as the word and the concept are essential to Scripture.

One Bible translator, John G. Paton, accidentally came upon a solution while hunting with a tribesman. The two men bagged a large deer and carried it on a pole along a steep mountain path to Paton's home. When they reached the veranda, both men dropped the load and plopped into the porch chairs. As they did so, the native exclaimed in the language of his people, "My, it is good to stretch yourself out here and rest." Paton immediately reached for paper and pencil and recorded the phrase.

As a result, his final translation of John 3:16 could be worded: "For God so loved the world, that he gave his only begotten Son, that whosoever stretcheth himself out on Him should not perish, but have everlasting life."[6]

Stretch out on Christ and rest.

Martin Luther did. When the great reformer was dying, severe headaches left him bedfast and pain struck. He was offered a medication to relieve the discomfort. He declined and explained, "My best prescription for head and heart is that *God so loved the world, that He gave His only begotten Son, that whosoever believeth in Him should not perish, but have everlasting life.*"[7]

The best prescription for head and heart. Who couldn't benefit from a dose? As things turned out, Nicodemus took his share. When Jesus was crucified, the theologian showed up with Joseph of Arimathea. The two offered their respects and oversaw Jesus's burial. No small gesture, given the anti-Christ climate of the day. When word hit the streets that Jesus was out of the tomb and back on his feet, don't you know Nicodemus smiled and thought of his late-night chat?

Born again, eh? Who would've thought he'd start with himself.

2

NO ONE LIKE HIM

"For God so loved the world . . ."

I *f only I could talk to the pilot.* Thirty seconds would do. Face-to-face. Just an explanation. He was, after all, the one bumping my wife and me from his plane.

Not that I could blame him. Denalyn had picked up more than souvenirs in Hong Kong. She was so nauseous I had to wheelchair her through the airport. She flopped onto her seat and pillowed her head against the window, and I promised to leave her alone for the fourteen-hour flight.

I had a simple goal: get Denalyn on the plane.

The airline staff had an opposite one: get Denalyn off.

Fault me for their fear. When a concerned flight attendant inquired about my wife's condition, I sent shock waves through the fuselage with my answer: "Virus." Attendants converged on our seats like police at a crime scene. Presidential news conferences have stirred fewer questions.

"How long has she been sick?"

"Did you see a doctor?"

"Have you considered swimming home?"

I downplayed Denalyn's condition. "Give us one barf bag, and we're happy travelers." No one laughed. Apparently bug-bearing patrons compete with terrorists for the title "Most Unwanted Passenger." The virus word reached the pilot, and the pilot rendered his verdict: "Not on my plane."

"You must leave," his bouncer informed matter-of-factly.

"Says who?"

"The pilot."

I leaned sideways and looked down the aisle for the man in charge, but the cockpit door was closed. *Coward.* If only I could talk to him, present my side. We didn't deserve banishment. We pay our taxes, vote in primaries, tip waiters. I wanted to plead my case, but the man in charge was unavailable for comment. He had a 747 to fly, seven thousand miles to navigate . . . and no time for us.

A few disheartening minutes later Denalyn and I found ourselves back at the gate, making plans to spend an extra night in China. As an airline representative made a list of hotel phone numbers, I noticed the plane pulling away. Hurrying over to the airport window, I stared into the cockpit, hoping for a glimpse of the mystery aviator. I waved both arms and mouthed my request: "Can we talk?" He didn't stop. I never saw his face. (But if you're reading this page, sir or ma'am, perhaps we could chat?)

Can you relate? You may feel similar sentiments about the pilot of the universe. God: the too-busy-for-you commander in chief, the faceless skipper who passes down nonnegotiable decisions. His universe hums like a Rolls-Royce, but sick passengers never appear on his radar screen. Even worse, you may suspect a vacant captain's seat. How do we know a hand secures the controls? Can we assume the presence of a pilot behind the steel door?

Christ weighs in decidedly on this discussion. He escorts passengers to the cockpit, enters 3:16 in the keypad, and unlocks the door to God. No Bible verse better expresses his nature. (We ought to submit it to *Webster's*.) Every word in the passage explains the second one. "For *God* so loved the world . . ."

Jesus assumes what Scripture declares: *God is.*

For proof, venture away from the city lights on a clear night and look up at the sky. That fuzzy band of white light is our galaxy, the Milky Way. One hundred billion stars.[1] Our galaxy is one of billions of others![2] Who can conceive of such a universe, let alone infinite numbers of universes?

No one can. But let's try anyway. Suppose you attempt to drive to the sun. A car dealer offers you a sweet deal on a space vehicle (no doubt solar powered) that averages 150 mph. You hop in, open the moonroof, and blast off. You drive nonstop, twenty-four hours a day, 365 days a year. Any guess as to the length of your trip? Try 70 years! Suppose, after stretching your legs and catching a bit of sun, you fuel up and rocket off to Alpha Centauri, the next closest star system. Best pack a lunch and clear your calendar. You'll need 15 million years to make the trip.[3]

Don't like to drive, you say? Board a jet, and zip through our solar system at a blistering 600 mph. In 16.5 days you'll reach the moon, in 17 years you'll pass the sun, and in 690 years you can enjoy dinner on Pluto. After seven centuries you haven't even left our solar system, much less our galaxy.[4]

Our universe is God's preeminent missionary. "The heavens declare the glory of God" (Ps. 19:1). A house implies a builder; a painting suggests a painter. Don't stars suggest a star maker?

Doesn't creation imply a creator? "The heavens declare His righteousness" (Ps. 97:6 NKJV). Look above you.

Now look within you. Look at your sense of right and wrong, your code of ethics. Somehow even as a child you knew it was wrong to hurt people and right to help them. Who told you? Who says? What is this magnetic pole that pulls the needles on the compass of your conscience if not God?

You aren't alone with your principles. Common virtues connect us. Every culture has frowned upon selfishness and celebrated courage, punished dishonesty and rewarded nobility. Even cannibals display rudimentary justice, usually refusing to eat their children.[5] A universal standard exists. Just as a code writer connects computers with common software bundles, a common code connects people. We may violate or ignore the code, but we can't deny it. Even people who have never heard God's name sense his law within them. "There is something deep within [humanity] that echoes God's yes and no, right and wrong" (Rom. 2:15 MSG). When atheists decry injustice, they can thank God for the ability to discern it. The conscience is God's fingerprint, proof of his existence.

Heavens above, moral code within—pings indicating the presence of an occupied cockpit. Someone got this plane airborne, and it wasn't any of us. There is a pilot, and he is unlike anyone we've seen.

"To whom, then, will you compare God?" the prophet invites (Isa. 40:18). To whom indeed? "Human hands can't serve his needs—for he has no needs" (Acts 17:25 NLT). You and I start our days needy. Indeed, basic needs prompt us to climb out of bed. Not God. Uncreated and self-sustaining, he depends on nothing and no one. Never taken a nap or a breath. Needs no food, counsel, or physician. "The Father has life in himself" (John 5:26). Life is to God what wetness is to water and air is to wind. He is not just alive but life itself. God is, without help.

Hence, he always is. "Before the mountains were brought forth, or ever You had formed the earth and the world, even from everlasting to everlasting, You are God" (Ps. 90:2 NKJV).

God never began and will never cease. He exists endlessly, always. "The number of His years is unsearchable" (Job 36:26 NASB).

Even so, let's try to search them. Let every speck of sand, from the Sahara to South Beach, represent a billion years of God's existence. With some super vacuum, suck and then blow all the particles into a mountain, and count how many you have. Multiply your total by a billion and listen as God reminds: "They don't represent a fraction of my existence."

He is "the eternal God" (Rom. 16:26). He invented time and owns the patent. "The day is yours, and yours also the night" (Ps. 74:16). He was something before anything else was. When the first angel lifted the first wing, God had already always been.

Most staggering of all, he has never messed up. Not once. The prophet Isaiah described his glimpse of God. He saw six-winged angels. Though sinless, they covered themselves in God's presence. Two wings covered eyes, two wings covered feet, and two carried the angels airborne. They volleyed one phrase back and forth: "Holy, holy, holy is the LORD of hosts" (Isa. 6:3 NKJV).

God is holy. Every decision, exact. Each word, appropriate. Never out-of-bounds or out of place. Not even tempted to make a mistake. "God is impervious to evil" (James 1:13 MSG).

Tally this up. No needs. No age. No sin. No wonder he said, "I am God, and there is none like me" (Isa. 46:9).

But is God's grandness good news? When Isaiah saw it, he came unraveled: "Woe is me, for I am undone!" (Isa. 6:5 NKJV). Competent pilots boot sick people off the plane. An all-powerful God might do likewise. Shouldn't the immensity of his universe intimidate us? It did Carl Sagan. A lifetime of studying the skies led the astronomer to conclude: "Our planet is a lonely speck in the great enveloping cosmic dark. In our obscurity, in all this vastness, there is no hint that help will come from elsewhere to save us from ourselves."[6]

Understandable pessimism. In the cockpit: God, who has no needs, age, or sin. Bouncing in the back of the plane: Max. Burger dependent. Half-asleep. Compared to God, I have the life span of a fruit fly. And sinless? I can't maintain a holy thought for my two-minute morning commute. Is God's greatness good news? Not without the next four words of John 3:16: "For God *so loved the world.*"

Try that mantra on for size. The one who holds the aces holds your heart. The one who formed you pulls for you. Untrumpable power stoked by unstoppable love. "If God is for us, who can be against us?" (Rom. 8:31).

God does for you what Bill Tucker's father did for him. Bill was sixteen years old when his dad suffered a health crisis and consequently had to leave his business. Even after Mr. Tucker regained his health, the Tucker family struggled financially, barely getting by.

Mr. Tucker, an entrepreneurial sort, came up with an idea. He won the bid to reupholster the chairs at the local movie theater. This stunned his family. He had never stitched a seat. He didn't even own a sewing apparatus. Still, he found someone to teach him the skill and located an industrial-strength machine. The family scraped together every cent they had to buy it. They drained savings accounts and dug coins out of the sofa. Finally they had enough.

It was a fine day when Bill rode with his dad to pick up the equipment. Bill remembers a jovial, hour-long trip discussing the bright horizons this new opportunity afforded them. They loaded the machine in the back of their truck and secured it right behind the cab. Mr. Tucker then invited his son to drive home. I'll let Bill tell you what happened:

"As we were driving along, we were excited, and I, like any sixteen-year-old driver, was probably not paying enough attention to my speed. Just as we were turning on the cloverleaf to get on the expressway, I will never ever, ever forget watching that sewing machine, which was already top-heavy, begin to tip. I slammed on the brakes, but it was too late. I saw it go over the side. I jumped out and ran around the back of the truck. As I rounded the corner, I saw our hope and our dream lying on its side in pieces. And then I saw my dad just looking. All of his risk and all of his endeavor and all of his struggling and all of his dream, all of his hope to take care of his family was lying there, shattered.

"You know what comes next, don't you? 'Stupid, punk kid driving too fast, not paying attention, ruined the family by taking away our livelihood.' But that's not what he said. He looked right at me. 'Oh, Bill, I am so sorry.' And he walked over, put his arms around me, and said, 'Son, this is going to be okay.'"[7]

God is whispering the same to you. Those are his arms you feel. Trust him. That is his voice you hear. Believe him. Allow the only decision maker in the universe to comfort you. Life at times appears to fall to pieces, seems irreparable. But it's going to be okay. How can you know? Because *God* so loved the world. And,

Since he has no needs, you cannot tire him.

Since he is without age, you cannot lose him.

Since he has no sin, you cannot corrupt him.

If God can make a billion galaxies, can't he make good out of our bad and sense out of our faltering lives? Of course he can. He is God. He not only flies the plane, but he knows the passengers and has a special place for those who are sick and ready to get home.

3

Hope for the Hard Heart

"For God so loved the world . . ."

I saw a woman today who finally became hard as wood all over." French physician Guy Patin wrote these words in 1692, the first clinical description of fibrodysplasia ossificans progressiva or FOP.

He unknowingly introduced the world to a cryptic disease that slowly, irreversibly turns its victims into a mass of solid bone.

Healthy skeletal systems are hinged together with ligaments and tendons. The bony figure hanging in the science classroom teaches this. Remove the connective tissues, and the frame collapses into a pile of loose bones.

FOP, however, hardens the soft tissues, like muscles and tendons, rendering the body an ossified suit of armor.

Consider the case of FOP victim Nancy Sando. When she was five, doctors diagnosed a mass on the back of her neck as terminal cancer and gave her three months to live. But she didn't die. No tumor grew. Her bones did, however. Doctors began to suspect the presence of the bone condition. By the time she was in her midthirties, her frame was frozen in a near-straight posture, mildly bent at the waist. Her neck was locked, jaw fused, and elbows fixed at right angles.

Injuries often trigger the FOP sprawl. Bones overreact to a bruise or break, spreading like renegade cement through the system. The pattern is predictable: neck and spine solidify first, then shoulders, hips, and elbows. Over years, the disease can imprison the entire body: back to front, head to toe, proximal to distal. The rogue gene of FOP has one aim: harden the body a little more every day.[1]

As tragic as this disease is, Scripture describes one even worse. The calcification, not of the bones, but of the will.

"I look at this people—oh! what a stubborn, hard-headed people!" (Exod. 32:9 MSG). God spoke these words to Moses on Mount Sinai. The disloyalty of the calf-worshiping Hebrews stunned God. He had given them a mayor's-seat perch at his Exodus extravaganza. They saw water transform into blood, high noon change to a midnight sky, the Red Sea turn into a red carpet, and the Egyptian army become fish bait. God gave manna with the morning dew, quail with the evening sun. He earned their trust. The former slaves had witnessed a millennium of miracles in a matter of days.

And yet, when God called Moses to a summit meeting, the people panicked like henless chicks. "They rallied around Aaron and said, 'Do something. Make gods for us who will lead us. That Moses, the man who got us out of Egypt—who knows what's happened to him?'" (Exod. 32:1 MSG).

The scurvy of fear infected everyone in the camp. They crafted a metal cow and talked to it. God, shocked at the calf-praising service, commanded Moses, "Go! Get down there! . . . They've turned away from the way I commanded them. . . . Oh! what a stubborn, hard-headed people!" (vv. 7–9 MSG).

Remember how FOP spreads in an unhealthy response to pain? Our hearts harden in an unhealthy reaction to fear. Note: the presence of fear in the Hebrews didn't bother God; their response to it did. Nothing persuaded the people to trust him. Plagues didn't. Liberation from slavery didn't. God shed light on their path and dropped food in their laps, and still they didn't believe him. Nothing penetrated their hearts. They were flinty. Stiff. Mount Rushmore is more pliable, an anvil more tender. The people were as responsive as the gold statue they worshiped.

More than three thousand years removed, we understand God's frustration. Turn to a statue for help? How stupid. Face your fears by facing a cow? *Udderly* foolish!

We opt for more sophisticated therapies: belly-stretching food binges or budget-busting shopping sprees. We bow before a whiskey bottle or lose ourselves in an eighty-hour work week. Progress? Hardly. We still face fears without facing God.

He sends Exodus-level demonstrations of power: sunsets, starry nights, immeasurable oceans. He solves Red Sea–caliber problems and air-drops blessings like morning manna. But let one crisis surface, let Moses disappear for a few hours, and we tornado into chaos. Rather than turn to God, we turn from him, hardening our hearts. The result? Cow-worshiping folly.

According to heaven's medical diagnosis:

[Hardhearted people] are hopelessly confused. Their minds are full of darkness; they wander far from the life God gives because they have closed their minds and *hardened their hearts against him*. They have no sense of shame. They live for lustful pleasure and eagerly practice every kind of impurity. (Eph. 4:17–19 NLT)

Measure the irregular pulse of the hard heart:
- "Hopelessly confused"
- "Minds . . . of darkness"
- "Have no sense of shame"
- "Live for lustful pleasure"
- "Practice every kind of impurity"

Morticians render a brighter diagnosis. No wonder Scripture says, "He who hardens his heart falls into trouble" (Prov. 28:14).

But it gets worse. A hard heart ruins, not only your life, but the lives of your family members. As an example, Jesus identified the hard heart as the wrecking ball of a marriage. When asked about divorce, Jesus said, "Moses permitted you to divorce your wives because your hearts were hard. But it was not this way from the beginning" (Matt. 19:8). When one or both people in a marriage stop trusting God to save it, they sign its death certificate. They reject the very one who can help them.

My executive assistant, Karen Hill, saw the result of such stubbornness in a pasture. A cow stuck her nose into a paint can and couldn't shake it off. Can-nosed cows can't breathe well, and they can't drink or eat at all. Both the cow and her calf were in danger. A serious bovine bind.

Karen's family set out to help. But when the cow saw the rescuers coming, she set out for pasture. They pursued, but the cow escaped. They chased that cow for three days! Each time the posse drew near, the cow ran. Finally, using pickup trucks and ropes, they cornered and de-canned the cow.

Seen any can-nosed people lately? Malnourished souls? Dehydrated hearts? People who can't take a deep breath? All because they stuck their noses where they shouldn't, and when God came to help, they ran away.

When billions of us imitate the cow, chaos erupts. Nations of bull-headed people ducking God and bumping into each other. We scamper, starve, and struggle.

Can-nosed craziness. Isn't this the world we see? This is the world God sees.

Yet, this is the world God loves. "For God so loved the world . . ." This hard-hearted, stiff-necked world. We bow before gold-plated cows; still, he loves us. We stick our noses where we shouldn't; still, he pursues us. We run from the very one who can help, but he doesn't give up. He loves. He pursues. He persists. And, every so often, a heart starts to soften.

Let yours be one of them. Here's how:

Don't forget what God has done for you. Jesus performed two bread-multiplying miracles: in one he fed five thousand people, in the other four thousand. Still, his disciples, who witnessed both feasts, worried about empty pantries. A frustrated Jesus rebuked them: "Are your hearts too hard to take it in? . . . Don't you remember anything at all?" (Mark 8:17–18 NLT).

Short memories harden the heart. Make careful note of God's blessings. Declare with David: "[I will] daily add praise to praise. I'll write the book on your righteousness, talk up your salvation the livelong day, never run out of good things to write or say" (Ps. 71:14–15 MSG).

Catalog God's goodnesses. Meditate on them. He has fed you, led you, and earned your trust. Remember what God has done for you. And,

Acknowledge what you have done against God. "If we claim we have not sinned, we are calling God a liar and showing that his word has no place in our hearts" (1 John 1:10 NLT).

Sin-hoarding stiffens us. Confession softens us.

When my daughters were small, they liked to play with Play-Doh. They formed figures out of the soft clay. If they forgot to place the lid on the can, the substance hardened. When it did, they brought it to me. My hands were bigger. My fingers stronger. I could mold the stony stuff into putty.

Is your heart hard? Take it to your Father. You're only a prayer away from tenderness. You live in a hard world, but you don't have to live with a hard heart.

4

WHEN YOU GET BOOTED OUT

"For God so loved *the world . . ."*

Pluto got bumped, cut from the first team, demoted from the top nine. According to a committee of scientists meeting in Prague, this outpost planet fails to meet solar-system standards. They downgraded the globe to asteroid #134340.[1] Believe me, Pluto was not happy. I caught up with the dissed sky traveler at a popular constellation hangout, the Night Sky Lounge.

MAX: Tell me, Pluto, how do you feel about the decision of the committee?

PLUTO: You mean those planet-pickers from Prague?

MAX: Yes.

PLUTO: I say no planet is perfect. Mars looks like a tanning-bed addict. Saturn has rings around the collar, and Jupiter moons everyone who passes.

MAX: So you don't approve of the decision?

PLUTO: (*snarling and whipping out a newspaper*) Who
comes up with these rules? *Too small. Wrong size
moon. Not enough impact.* Do they know how hard
it is to hang on at the edge of the solar system?
They think I'm spacey. Let them duck meteors
coming at them at thousands of miles per hour for
a few millennia, and then see who they call a
planet. I'm outta here. I can take the hint. I know
when I'm not wanted. Walt Disney named a dog
after me. Teachers always put me last on the
science quiz. Darth Vader gives me more respect.
I'm joining up with a meteor shower. Tell that
committee to keep an eye on the night sky. I know
where they live.

Can't fault Pluto for being ticked. One day he's in, the next
he's out; one day on the squad, the next off. We can understand
his frustration. Some of us understand it all too well. We know
what it's like to be voted out. Wrong size. Wrong crowd. Wrong
address.

Plutoed.

To the demoted and demeaned, Jesus directs his leadoff verb.
"For God so *loved* the world . . ." *Love.* We've all but worn out
the word. This morning I used *love* to describe my feelings toward
my wife and toward peanut butter. Far from identical emotions.
I've never proposed to a jar of peanut butter (though I have let
one sit on my lap during a television show). Overuse has defused
the word, leaving it with the punch of a butterfly wing.

Biblical options still retain their starch. Scripture employs an
artillery of terms for love, each one calibrated to reach a differ-

ent target. Consider the one Moses used with his followers: "The LORD chose your ancestors as the objects of his love" (Deut. 10:15 NLT).

This passage warms our hearts. But it shook the Hebrews' world. They heard this: "The Lord binds [*hasaq*] himself to his people." *Hasaq* speaks of a tethered love, a love attached to something or someone.[2] I'm picturing a mom connected by a child harness to her rambunctious five-year-old as the two of them walk through the market. (I once thought the leashes were cruel; then I became a dad.) The strap serves two functions, yanking and claiming. You yank your kid out of trouble and in doing so proclaim, "Yes, he is as wild as a banshee. But he's mine."

In this case, God chained himself to Israel. Because the people were lovable? No. "GOD wasn't attracted to you and didn't choose you because you were big and important—the fact is, there was almost nothing to you. He did it out of sheer love, keeping the promise he made to your ancestors" (Deut. 7:7–8 MSG). God loves Israel and the rest of us Plutos because he chooses to. "This is the love that won't let go of the object of love."[3]

George Matheson learned to depend on this love. He was only a teenager when doctors told him he was going blind. Not to be denied, he pursued his studies, graduating from the University of Glasgow in 1861 at the age of nineteen. By the time he finished graduate seminary studies, he was sightless.

His fiancée returned his engagement ring with a note: "I cannot see my way clear to go through life bound by the chains of marriage to a blind man."

Matheson never married. He adapted to his sightless world but never recovered from his broken heart. He became a powerful and poetic pastor, led a full and inspiring life. Yet occasionally the pain of his unrequited affection flared up, as it did decades later at his sister's wedding. The ceremony brought back memories of the love he had lost. In response, he turned to the unending love of God for comfort and penned these words on June 6, 1882:

> O love that wilt not let me go, I rest my weary soul in thee; I give thee back the life I owe, that in thine ocean depths its flow may richer, fuller be.[4]

God will not let you go. He has handcuffed himself to you in love. And he owns the only key. You need not win his love. You already have it. And since you can't win it, you can't lose it.

As evidence, consider exhibit A: the stubborn love of Hosea for Gomer. Contrary to the name, Gomer was a female, an irascible woman married to a remarkable Hosea. She had the fidelity code of a prairie jackrabbit, flirting and hopping from one lover to another. She ruined her life and shattered Hosea's heart. Destitute, she was placed for sale in a slave market. Guess who stepped forward to buy her? Hosea, who'd never removed his wedding band. The way he treated her you would have thought she'd never loved another man. God uses this story, indeed orchestrated this drama, to illustrate his steadfast love for his fickle people.

> Then GOD ordered [Hosea], "Start all over: Love your wife again,
>> your wife who's in bed with her latest boyfriend,
>> your cheating wife.
> Love her the way I, GOD, love the Israelite people,

even as they flirt and party with every god that takes
their fancy."
(Hosea 3:1 MSG)

This is the love described in John 3:16. *Hasaq* is replaced with
the Greek term *agape,* but the meaning is equally powerful.
"God so [*agapao*] the world . . ."

Agape love. Less an affection, more a decision; less a feeling, more an action. As one linguist describes, "[Agape love is]
an exercise of the Divine will in deliberate choice, made without assignable cause save that which lies in the nature of God
Himself."[5]

Stated more simply: junkyard wrecks and showroom models
share equal space in God's garage.

I saw a shard of such love between an elderly man and woman
who have been married for fifty years. The last decade has been
marred by her dementia. The husband did the best he could to
care for his wife at home, but she grew sicker; he, older. So he
admitted her to full-time care.

One day he asked me to visit her, so I did. Her room was
spotless, thanks to his diligence. She, horizontal on the bed, was
bathed and dressed, though going nowhere.

"I arrive at 6:15 a.m.," he beamed. "You'd think I was on the
payroll. I feed her, bathe her, and stay with her. I will until one
of us dies." Agape love.

I know a father who, out of love for his son, spends each
night in a recliner, never sleeping more than a couple of consecutive hours. A car accident paralyzed the teenager. To maintain the
boy's circulation, therapists massage his limbs every few hours. At
night the father takes the place of the therapists. Though he's

worked all day and will work again the next, he sets the alarm to wake himself every other hour until sunrise.

Then there is the story Dan Mazzeo tells about his father: "Pop," a first-generation Italian American who was struggling with metastatic liver and lung cancer. When doctors gave him less than a year, Pop bravely said he wasn't afraid to die. After all, his wife was already gone and his children grown. But then he learned that his only son, Dan, was going to be a father. When Pop heard the news, he sat up and resolved, "I'm gonna make that."

The chemo tortured his system. Some days it was all he could do to mumble, "Bad day," to those who phoned. But when his granddaughter was born, he insisted on going to the hospital. The ninety-minute ride tormented him. Dan wheeled him to the maternity ward. Pop's arms were too weak, so Dan had to hold the baby for him. But Pop did what he came to do. He leaned over, kissed her, and said, "Sheila Mary, Grandpa loves you very much."

Within seconds, Pop dozed off. Within an hour he was back in the car. Within days he was dead.[6]

What is this love that endures decades, passes on sleep, and resists death to give one kiss? Call it agape love, a love that bears a semblance of God's.

But only a semblance, mind you, never a replica. Our finest love is a preschool watercolor to God's Rembrandt, a vacant-lot dandelion next to his garden rose. His love stands sequoia strong; our best attempts bend like weeping willows.

We may bathe an aging bride, massage a boy, or issue a final blessing, but compare our love with God's? Look at the round belly of the pregnant peasant girl in Bethlehem. God's in there;

the same God who can balance the universe on the tip of his finger floats in Mary's womb. Why? Love.

Peek through the Nazareth workshop window. See the lanky
lad sweeping the sawdust from the floor? He once blew stardust
into the night sky. Why swap the heavens for a carpentry shop?
One answer: love.

Love explains why he came.

Love explains how he endured.

His hometown kicked him out. A so-called friend turned
him in. Hucksters called God a hypocrite. Sinners called God
guilty. Do termites mock an eagle, tapeworms decry the beauty
of a swan? How did Jesus endure such derision? "For God so
loved . . ."

"Observe how Christ loved us. . . . He didn't love in order to
get something from us but to give everything of himself to us"
(Eph. 5:2 MSG).

Your goodness can't win God's love. Nor can your badness
lose it. But you can resist it. We tend to do so honestly. Having
been Plutoed so often, we fear God may Pluto us as well.
Rejections have left us skittish and jumpy. Like my dog Salty.

He sleeps next to me on the couch as I write. He's a cranky
cuss, but I like him. We've aged together over the last fifteen
years, and he seems worse for the wear. He's a wiry canine by
nature; shave his salt-and-pepper mop, and he'd pass for a bulimic
Chihuahua. He didn't have much to start with; now the seasons
have taken his energy, teeth, hearing, and all but eighteen inches'
worth of eyesight.

Toss him a dog treat, and he just stares at the floor through
cloudy cataracts. (Or, in his case, dogaracts?) He's nervous and
edgy, quick to growl and slow to trust. As I reach out to pet him,

he yanks back. Still, I pet the old coot. I know he can't see, and I can only wonder how dark his world has become.

We are a lot like Salty. I have a feeling that most people who defy and deny God do so more out of fear than conviction. For all our chest pumping and braggadocio, we are anxious folk— can't see a step into the future, can't hear the one who owns us. No wonder we try to gum the hand that feeds us.

But God reaches and touches. He speaks through the immensity of the Russian plain and the density of the Amazon rain forest. Through a physician's touch in Africa, a bowl of rice in India. Through a Japanese bow or a South American *abraço*. He's even been known to touch people through paragraphs like the ones you are reading. If he is touching you, let him.

Mark it down: God loves you with an unearthly love. You can't win it by being winsome. You can't lose it by being a loser. But you can be blind enough to resist it.

Don't. For heaven's sake, don't. For your sake, don't.

"Take in with all Christians the extravagant dimensions of Christ's love. Reach out and experience the breadth! Test its length! Plumb the depths! Rise to the heights! Live full lives, full in the fullness of God" (Eph. 3:18–19 MSG). Others demote you. God claims you. Let the definitive voice of the universe say, "You're still a part of my plan."

5

THE ONLY ONE AND ONLY

". . . he gave his one and only Son . . ."

Two of our three daughters were born in the South Zone of Rio de Janeiro, Brazil. We lived in the North Zone, separated from our doctor's office and hospital by a tunnel-pierced mountain range. During Denalyn's many months of pregnancy, we made the drive often.

We didn't complain. Signs of life do a samba on every street corner. Copacabana and her bathers. Ipanema and her coffee bars. Gavea and her glamour. We never begrudged the South Zone forays. But they sure did bewilder me. I kept getting lost. I'm directionally challenged anyway, prone to take a wrong turn between the bedroom and bathroom. Complicate my disorientation with randomly mapped three-hundred-year-old streets, and I don't stand a chance.

I had one salvation. Jesus. Literally, Jesus. The Christ the Redeemer statue. The figure stands guard over the city, one hundred and twenty-five feet tall with an arm span of nearly a hundred feet. More than a thousand tons of reinforced steel. The head alone measures ten feet from chin to scalp. Perched a mile and a half above sea level on Corcovado Mountain, the elevated Jesus is always visible. Especially to those who are looking for it. Since I was often lost, I was often looking. As a sailor seeks land, I searched for the statue, peering between the phone lines and rooftops for the familiar face. Find him and find my bearings.

John 3:16 offers you an identical promise. The verse elevates Christ to thin-air loftiness, crowning him with the most regal of titles: "One and Only Son."

The Greek word for "one and only" is *monogenes,*[1] an adjective compounded of *monos* ("only") and *genes* ("species, race, family, offspring, kind"). When used in the Bible, "one and only" almost always describes a parent-child relationship. Luke employs it to identify the widow's son: "the only son of his mother" (Luke 7:12 ESV). The writer of Hebrews states, "Abraham . . . was ready to sacrifice his only son, Isaac" (11:17 NLT).

John enlists the phrase five times, in each case highlighting the unparalleled relationship between Jesus and God:

1. The Word became flesh and made his dwelling among us. We have seen his glory, the glory of *the One and Only,* who came from the Father, full of grace and truth. (John 1:14)

2. No one has ever seen God, but God *the One and Only,* who is at the Father's side, has made him known. (John 1:18)

3. For God so loved the world that he gave his *one and only Son.* (John 3:16)

4. Whoever believes in him is not condemned, but whoever does not believe stands condemned already because he has not believed in the name of God's *one and only* Son. (John 3:18)
5. This is how God showed his love among us: He sent his *one and only* Son into the world that we might live through him. (1 John 4:9)

In three of the five appearances, the phrase modifies the noun *Son.* In the two cases it doesn't, the Son was either "from the Father" or "at the Father's side" (John 1:14, 18 ESV).

Monogenes, then, highlights the particular relationship between Jesus and God. Though God is the father of all humanity, Jesus alone is the *monogenetic* Son of God, because only Christ has God's genes or genetic makeup.

The familiar translation "only begotten Son" (John 3:16 NKJV, NASB) conveys this truth. When parents beget or conceive a child, they transfer their DNA to the newborn. Jesus shares God's DNA. Jesus isn't begotten in the sense that he began but in the sense that he and God have the same essence, eternal life span, unending wisdom, and tireless energy. Every quality we attribute to God, we can attribute to Jesus.

"Anyone who has seen me has seen the Father!" Jesus claimed (John 14:9 NLT). And the epistle to the Hebrews concurs: "[Christ] is the radiance of [God's] glory and the exact representation of His nature" (1:3 NASB).

Jesus occupies the peerless "Christ the Redeemer" pedestal. He claims, not the most authority, but all authority. "My Father has given me authority over everything. No one really knows the Son except the Father, and no one really knows the Father except

3:16

THE NUMBERS OF HOPE

MAX LUCADO

THOMAS NELSON
Since 1798

NASHVILLE DALLAS MEXICO CITY RIO DE JANEIRO BEIJING

the Son and those to whom the Son chooses to reveal him" (Matt. 11:27 NLT).

Don't hurry through those words. They're either the last straw or the ultimate truth. They warrant deliberate thought.

"My Father has given me authority over everything." Does Jesus own the only scepter in the universe? One follower declared as much. A Roman officer sent a message to Jesus, asking the teacher to heal his servant. So Jesus journeyed toward the soldier's house. But the man sent friends to intercept Jesus, telling him not to make an unnecessary trip. "Just say the word from where you are, and my servant will be healed. I know this because I am under the authority of my superior officers, and I have authority over my soldiers. I only need to say, 'Go,' and they go, or 'Come,' and they come. And if I say to my slaves, 'Do this,' they do it" (Luke 7:7–8 NLT).

This officer understood authority: when the one in charge commands, the ones beneath obey. The soldier effectively said, "Jesus, you call the shots, inhabit the throne. You wear five stars on your shoulder." He saluted Christ as supreme commander.

And Christ didn't correct him! Jesus didn't dilute the man's opinion or adjust his comments. "You flatter me," he could have said. But he didn't dismiss the adulation as overstatement; rather he accepted it as appropriate. "I tell you, I haven't seen faith like this in all Israel!" (v. 9 NLT).

Christ claims ultimate clout. Unshared supremacy. He steers the ship and pilots the plane. When he darts his eyes, oceans swell. When he clears his throat, birds migrate. He banishes bacteria with a single thought. "He sustains everything by the mighty power of his command" (Heb. 1:3 NLT).

He is to history what a weaver is to a tapestry. I once watched a weaver work at a downtown San Antonio market. She selected threads from her bag and arranged them first on the frame, then on the shuttle. She next worked the shuttle back and forth over the threads, intertwining colors, overlapping textures. In a matter of moments a design appeared.

Christ, in like manner, weaves his story. Every person is a thread, every moment a color, every era a pass of the shuttle. Jesus steadily interweaves the embroidery of humankind. "'My thoughts are nothing like your thoughts,' says the LORD. 'And my ways are far beyond anything you could imagine'" (Isa. 55:8 NLT). A root meaning of the word translated *thoughts* is "artistic craftmanship."[2] As if God says, "My artistry is far beyond anything you could imagine."

Christ: the One and Only Ruler. The One and Only Ruler then claims to be the One and Only Revealer. "No one really knows the Son except the Father, and no one really knows the Father except the Son" (Matt. 11:27 NLT).

Jesus enjoys an intimacy with God, a mutuality the Father shares with no one else.

Married couples know something of this. They finish each other's sentences, anticipate each other's actions. Some even begin to look like each other (a possibility that deeply troubles my wife).

Denalyn and I have been married more than twenty-five years. We no longer converse; we communicate in code. She walks into the kitchen while I'm making a sandwich.

"Denalyn?" I ask.

"No, I don't want one."

I'll open the fridge and stare for a few moments. "Denalyn?"

She'll look at my sandwich preparations and answer, "Mayo on the top shelf. Pickles on the door."

She knows what I'll say before I say it. Consequently, she can speak on my behalf with highest credibility. If she says, "Max would prefer a different color" or "Max would approve this idea," listen to her. She knows what she's talking about. She qualifies as my proxy like no one else.

How much more does Jesus qualify as God's! Jesus "who exists at the very heart of the Father, has made him plain as day" (John 1:18 MSG).

When Jesus says, "In My Father's house are many mansions" (John 14:2 NKJV), count on it. He knows. He has walked them.

When he says, "You are worth more than many sparrows" (Matt. 10:31), trust him. Jesus knows. He knows the value of every creature.

When Christ declares, "Your Father knows what you need before you ask him" (Matt. 6:8 NAB), believe it. After all, "He was in the beginning with God" (John 1:2 NAB).

Jesus claims to be, not a *top* theologian, an *accomplished* theologian, or even the *Supreme* Theologian, but rather the *Only* Theologian. "No one really knows the Father except the Son." He does not say, "No one really knows the Father *like* the Son" or "*in the fashion* of the Son." But rather, "No one really knows the Father except the Son."

Heaven's door has one key, and Jesus holds it.

Think of it this way. You're a fifth grader studying astronomy. The day you read about the first mission to the moon, you and your classmates pepper the teacher with space-travel questions.

"What does moondust feel like?"

"Can you swallow when there's no gravity?"

"What about going to the bathroom?"

The teacher does the best she can but prefaces most replies with "I would guess . . ." or "I think . . ." or "Perhaps . . ."

How could she know? She's never been there. But the next day she brings a guest who has. Neil Armstrong enters the room. Yes, the "one small step for man, one giant leap for mankind" Neil Armstrong.

"Now ask your questions," the teacher invites. And Astronaut Armstrong answers each with certainty. He knows the moon; he's walked on it. No speculation or hesitation—he speaks with conviction.

So did Jesus. "He was teaching them as one who had authority" (Matt. 7:29 ESV). Jesus knows the dimensions of God's throne room, the fragrance of its incense, the favorite songs of the unceasing choir. He has a unique, one-of-a-kind, unrivaled knowledge of God and wants to share his knowledge with you. "No one really knows the Father except the Son and those *to whom the Son chooses to reveal him*" (Matt. 11:27 NLT).

Jesus doesn't boast in his knowledge; he shares it. He doesn't gloat; he gives. He doesn't revel; he reveals. He reveals to us the secrets of eternity.

And he shares them, not just with the top brass or purebred, but with the hungry and needy. In the very next line, Jesus invites: "Come to me, all of you who are weary and carry heavy burdens, and I will give you rest. Take my yoke upon you. Let me teach you, because I am humble and gentle at heart, and you will find rest for your souls" (vv. 28–29 NLT).

Do yourself a favor. Find the brightest highlighter manufactured and the darkest ink produced. Underscore, underline, and accept his invitation: "Let me teach you . . ."

One of my Boy Scout assignments was to build a kite. One of

my blessings as a Boy Scout was a kite-building dad. He built a lot of things: scooters on skates, go-carts. Why, he even built our house. A kite to him was stick figures to Van Gogh. Could handle them in his sleep.

With wood glue, poles, and newspaper, we fashioned a sky-dancing masterpiece: red, white, and blue, and shaped like a box. We launched our creation on the back of a March wind. But after some minutes, my kite caught a downdraft and plunged. I tightened the string, raced in reverse, and did all I could to maintain elevation. But it was too late. She Hindenburged earthward.

Envision a redheaded, heartsick twelve-year-old standing over his collapsed kite. That was me. Envision a square-bodied man with ruddy skin and coverall, placing his hand on the boy's shoulder. That was my kite-making dad. He surveyed the heap of sticks and paper and assured, "It's okay. We can fix this." I believed him. Why not? He spoke with authority.

So does Christ. To all whose lives feel like a crashed kite, he says, "We can fix this. Let me teach you. Let me teach you how to handle your money, long Mondays, and cranky in-laws. Let me teach you why people fight, death comes, and forgiveness counts. But most of all, let me teach you why on earth you are on this earth."

Don't we need to learn? We know so much, and yet we know so little. The age of information is the age of confusion: much know-how, hardly any know-why. We need answers. Jesus offers them.

But can we trust him? Only one way to know. Do what I did in Rio. Seek him out. Lift up your eyes, and set your sights on Jesus. No passing glances or occasional glimpses. Enroll in his school. "Let me teach you . . ." Make him your polestar, your point of reference. Search the crowded streets and shadow-casting roofs until you spot his face, and then set your sights on him.

You'll find more than a hospital.

You'll find the Only One and Only.

6

THE HEART
HE OFFERS

"... he gave his one and only Son ..."

As far as medical exams are concerned, this one was simple. As far as I'm concerned, no exam is simple if it couples the word *irregular* with *heartbeat*. I knew I was prone to have an accelerated pulse. When I see Denalyn, my ticker ramps up. When Denalyn brings me a bowl of ice cream, you'd think a Geiger counter had struck pay dirt in my chest.

Such palpitations are to be expected. It was the random rhythms that concerned the cardiologist. You won't find a kinder physician. He did his best to assure me that, as far as heart conditions go, mine isn't serious: "When it comes to cardiac concerns, you've got the best kind."

Forgive my anemic enthusiasm. But isn't that like telling the about-to-leap paratrooper, "Your parachute has a defect, but it's not the worst type"? I prefer the treatment of another heart doctor. He saw my condition and made this eye-popping offer: "Let's exchange hearts. Mine is sturdy; yours is frail. Mine pure, yours diseased. Take mine and enjoy its vigor. Give me yours. I'll endure its irregularity."

Where do you find such a physician? You can reach him at this number—3:16. At the heart of this verse, he deals with the heart of our problem: "For God so loved the world that he *gave* his one and only Son."

"That's the craziest claim I've ever heard," a man once told me. He and I shared a row and a meal on an airplane. But we did not share an appreciation for John 3:16.

"I don't need God to *give* anyone for me," he claimed. "I've led a good life. Held a good job. People respect me. My wife loves me. I don't need God to give me his son."

Perhaps you agree. You appreciate the teachings of Jesus. Admire his example. But no matter how you turn it around, you can't see the significance of his death. How can the death of Christ mean life for us? The answer begins with a heart exam.

"The heart is deceitful above all things, and desperately wicked" (Jer. 17:9 NKJV). The Spiritual Cardiologist scans our hearts and finds deep disease: "For from within, out of men's hearts, come evil thoughts, sexual immorality, theft, murder, adultery, greed, malice, deceit, lewdness, envy, slander, arrogance and folly" (Mark 7:21–22). He describes our problem in pandemic proportions: "No one is righteous—not even one. No one is truly wise; no one is seeking God" (Rom. 3:10–11 NLT).

Surely this is an overstatement, an exaggeration. Can it be that "we are utterly incapable of living the glorious lives God wills for us" (Rom. 3:23 MSG)?

This generation is oddly silent about sin. Late-night talk shows don't discuss humanity's shortcomings. Some mental-health professionals mock our need for divine forgiveness. At the same time, we rape the earth, squander nonrenewable resources, and let 24,000 people die daily from hunger or hunger-related causes.[1] In these "modern" decades we have invented global threat, reinvented genocide and torture. The twentieth century saw more slaughters than any other century in history—from the Ottoman massacre of 1.5 million Armenians in World War I to the 1990s slaughter of 3 million people in Rwanda and Sudan. Lurking between them: the Ukraine terror famine, Auschwitz, the rape of Nanking, the Burma railway, Soviet Gulag, Chinese Cultural Revolution, Cambodian killing fields, Yugoslavian and Bangladesh slaughters. Wars and genocides took more than 200 million souls in one hundred years![2]

Barbarism apparently is alive and well on the planet Earth. Deny our sin? Quasimodo could more easily deny his hump. Our heart problem? It's universal.

And personal. Do a simple exercise with me. Measure your life against these four standards from the Ten Commandments. Heaven's applicants should score well on God's basic laws, wouldn't you agree?

1. "You must not steal" (Exod. 20:15 TLB). Have you ever stolen anything? A paper clip, parking place? Thief.
2. "You must not lie" (v. 16 TLB). Those who say they haven't just did.
3. "You must not commit adultery" (v. 14 TLB). Jesus said if you look at a woman with lust, you've committed adultery in your heart (Matt. 5:28).
4. "You must not murder" (v. 13 TLB). Before you claim innocence, remember, Jesus equates murder with anger. "Anyone who is so much as angry with a brother or sister

is guilty of murder" (Matt. 5:22 MSG). We assassinate a dozen drivers on the morning commute.

Bad news from the Cardiologist. Your test score indicts you as a thieving, lying, adulterous murderer.

Contrast your heart with Christ's. When you list the claims that qualify him as either crazy or kingly, don't omit this one: he asserted to have the only sinless heart in all of history. He invited, "Can any one of you convict me of a single misleading word, a single sinful act?" (John 8:46 MSG). Issue that challenge to my friends, and hands will wave like stalks in a Kansas wheat field. In response to Jesus's challenge, however, no one could convict him of sin. His enemies drummed up false charges in order to arrest him. Pilate, the highest-ranking official in the region, found no guilt in Jesus. Peter, who walked in Jesus's shadow for three years, recorded: "He never did one thing wrong, not once said anything amiss" (1 Pet. 2:22 MSG).

Jesus's standard mutes all boasting.

I experienced a remotely similar standard when I met golf legend Byron Nelson. Brand-new to the game, I had just broken a hundred on the golf course for the first time. A friend had an appointment with Mr. Nelson and asked me to come along. En route I bragged about my double-digit score, offering a hole-by-hole summary. Fearing I might do the same with the retired icon, my friend asked what I knew of Byron Nelson's accomplishments, and then he told me:

- five major titles
- eleven consecutive victories
- an average score of sixty-nine during the streak

My score of ninety-eight seemed suddenly insignificant. Mr. Nelson's standard silenced me. Jesus's perfection silences us.

So how does he respond to our unholy hearts? Can a good cardiologist spot irregularity and dismiss it? Can God overlook our sins as innocent mistakes? No. He is the one and only judge. He issues decrees, not opinions; commands, not suggestions. They are truth. They emerge from his holy self. Violate them, and you dethrone him—dethrone him at the highest cost.

Jesus made his position clear: "Anyone whose life is not holy will never see the Lord" (Heb. 12:14 NCV). Hard-hearted souls will not populate heaven.

It is the "pure in heart" who will "see God" (Matt. 5:8). So where does that leave us? It leaves us drawing hope from a five-letter Greek word.

Hyper means "in place of" or "on behalf of."[3] New Testament writers repeatedly turned to this preposition to describe the work of Christ:

- "Christ died for [*hyper*] our sins . . ." (1 Cor. 15:3).
- "Jesus gave himself for [*hyper*] our sins" (Gal. 1:4 NCV).
- "Christ redeemed us from the curse of the Law, having become a curse for [*hyper*] us" (Gal. 3:13 NASB).
- Jesus himself prophesied: "The good shepherd lays down his life for [*hyper*] the sheep" (John 10:11).
- "Greater love has no one than this, that he lay down his life for [*hyper*] his friends" (John 15:13).
- Before his death, Jesus took bread and explained: "This is my body given for [*hyper*] you" (Luke 22:19). And presenting the cup, he explained: "This cup is the new

covenant in my blood, which is poured out for [*hyper*] you" (v. 20).

For sounding hyper about *hyper,* I apologize, but the point is crucial. Christ exchanged hearts with you. Yes, your thieving, lying, adulterous, and murderous heart. He placed your sin in himself and invited God to punish it. "The LORD has put on him the punishment for all the evil we have done" (Isa. 53:6 NCV).

A Chinese Christian understood this point. Before her baptism, a pastor asked a question to ensure she understood the meaning of the cross. "Did Jesus have any sin?" he inquired.

"Yes," she replied.

Troubled, he repeated the question.

"He had sin," she answered positively.

The leader set out to correct her, but she insisted, "He had mine."[4]

Though healthy, Jesus took our disease upon himself. Though diseased, we who accept his offer are pronounced healthy. More than pardoned, we are declared innocent. We enter heaven, not with healed hearts, but with his heart. It is as if we have never sinned. Read slowly the announcement of Paul: "If anyone is in Christ, he is a new creation; the old has gone, the new has come!" (2 Cor. 5:17).

We enjoy the same status as Bertram Campbell. He spent three years and four months in prison for a forgery he did not commit. When the real criminal finally confessed, the governor declared Campbell, not just pardoned, but innocent.[5] God does for us exactly the same. "God made him who had no sin to be sin for us, so that in him we might become the righteousness of God" (2 Cor. 5:21).

This is no transplant, mind you, but a swap. The holy and the vile exchange locations. God makes healthy what was sick, right what was wrong, straight what was crooked.

Steven Vryhof witnessed the impact of this gift in a Lutheran church on the coast of Sweden. A handful of the faithful had gathered to sing, pray, and celebrate communion. He took his turn at the altar, received the bread and the wine, and returned to his seat.

As the minister turned his back to the congregation and began putting away the elements, two more worshippers came forward. A middle-aged woman pushed her mother in a wheelchair. "The mother," writes Vryhof, "had the classic nursing-home look: slumped to the right, thin, scraggly, colorless hair, vacant eyes, and a slack-jaw with her tongue showing a bit. She was here for communion."

Everyone but the minister knew of the two women at the altar. When he finally realized their presence, he retrieved the elements and administered the piece of bread and the sip of wine. He then paused, looked the old woman directly in the eye, and declared the customary blessing: "Our Lord Jesus Christ, whose body and blood you have received, preserve your soul unto everlasting life."

The irony struck Vryhof. The woman was too old to keep her balance or her head straight. She brought nothing but a bent body and feeble bones. Dare one believe that heaven cares for such a soul? The moment Vryhof asked the question, the church bells erupted, pealing, ringing unexpectedly and majestically. It was as if God himself was declaring, "I will claim the frail, preserve the weak, and secure the weary. Let them come."[6]

And so we do. Scarred and journey-hardened, we come. "Can you do something with this heart?" we ask.

He nods and smiles. "Suppose we discuss a swap."

7

HEAVEN'S "WHOEVER" POLICY

*". . . whoever believes in him
shall not perish . . ."*

waterway with a time capsule interred in her base. Someday, city officials reasoned, when Britain goes the way of ancient Egypt, excavators will open the box to find a slice of Victorian England. They'll discover a set of coins, children's toys, a city directory, photographs of the twelve most beautiful women of the day, a razor, and, in 215 languages, a verse from the Bible: "For God so loved the world that he gave his one and only son, that whoever believes in him shall not perish but have eternal life."[1]

Picture a rummager of some future London digging through rocks and rubble. She finds and reads the verse. Except for one word, she might dismiss it as an old myth. *Whoever.*

Whoever unfurls 3:16 as a banner for the ages. *Whoever* unrolls the welcome mat of heaven to humanity. *Whoever* invites the world to God.

Jesus could have so easily narrowed the scope, changing *whoever* into *whatever.* "Whatever Jew believes" or "Whatever woman follows me." But he used no qualifier. The pronoun is wonderfully indefinite. After all, who isn't a *whoever*?

The word sledgehammers racial fences and dynamites social classes. It bypasses gender borders and surpasses ancient traditions. *Whoever* makes it clear: God exports his grace worldwide. For those who attempt to restrict it, Jesus has a word: *Whoever.*

Whoever acknowledges me before men, I will also acknowledge him before my Father in heaven. (Matt. 10:32)

Whoever finds his life will lose it, and *whoever* loses his life for my sake will find it. (Matt. 10:39)

Whoever does God's will is my brother and sister and mother. (Mark 3:35)

Whoever believes and is baptized will be saved, but *whoever* does not believe will be condemned. (Mark 16:16)

Whoever believes in the Son has eternal life, but *whoever* rejects the Son will not see life, for God's wrath remains on him. (John 3:36)

Whoever drinks the water I give him will never thirst. (John 4:14)

Whoever comes to me I will never drive away. (John 6:37)

Whoever lives and believes in me will never die. (John 11:26)

Whoever is thirsty, let him come; and *whoever* wishes, let him take the free gift of the water of life. (Rev. 22:17)

Titus 2:11 assures us that "the grace of God . . . has appeared to all men." Paul contends that Jesus Christ sacrificed himself "to win freedom for all mankind" (1 Tim. 2:6 NEB). Peter affirms that "it is not his [God's] will for any to be lost, but for all to come to repentance" (2 Pet. 3:9 NEB). God's gospel has a "whoever" policy.

We need to know this. The downturns of life can create such a sad state of affairs that we wonder if God still wants us. Surely Lazarus the beggar wondered. Jesus tells us this about him:

There was a rich man who was dressed in purple and fine linen and lived in luxury every day. At his gate was laid a beggar named Lazarus, covered with sores and longing to eat what fell from the rich man's table. Even the dogs came and licked his sores. (Luke 16:19–21)

The two men indwell opposite sides of the city tracks. The rich man lives in posh luxury and wears the finest clothing. The language suggests he uses fabric worth its weight in gold.[2] He eats exotic food, enjoys a spacious house with botanical gardens. He's the New Testament version of a Monaco billionaire.

Lazarus is a homeless street sleeper. Dogs lick the sores that cavern his skin. He languishes outside the mansion, hoping for scraps. Infected. Rejected. No possessions. No family. An exception to God's "whoever" policy, right?

Wrong.

In sudden drama, the curtain of death falls on act 1, and eternal destiny is revealed in act 2.

The time came when the beggar died and the angels carried him to Abraham's side. The rich man also died and was buried. In hell, where he was in torment, he looked up and saw Abraham far away, with Lazarus by his side. (vv. 22–23)

Just-poor Lazarus now needs nothing. The now-poor rich man needs everything. He loses the lap of luxury, and Lazarus discovers the lap of Abraham.

Lazaruses still populate our planet. You may be one. Not begging for bread, but struggling to buy some. Not sleeping on streets, but on the floor perhaps? In your car sometimes?

On a couch often? Does God have a place for people in your place?

Of all the messages this account conveys, don't miss this one: God takes you *however* he finds you. No need to clean up or climb up. Just look up. God's "whoever" policy has a "however" benefit.

It also features a "whenever" clause. *Whenever* you hear God's voice, he welcomes your response. While cleaning my car, I found a restaurant gift certificate. Amid the papers, gum wrappers, and trash was a treasure: fifty dollars' worth of food. I'd received it for my birthday over a year ago and had misplaced it. My enthusiasm was short-lived when I saw the expiration date. The invitation had expired. I had waited too long.

But you haven't. And to convince you, Jesus wove a parable of eleventh-hour grace. He described a landowner who needed helpers. Just as a farmer hires migrant workers or a landscaper fills a crew with temps, this man employed workers. "They agreed on a wage of a dollar a day, and went to work" (Matt. 20:2 MSG). A few were hired early in the morning. Others at 9:00 a.m. The landowner recruited a few more at noon. Came back at 3:00 p.m. for more. And at 5:00 p.m., one hour before quitting time, he picked up one more truckload.

Those last men were surely surprised. One hour remaining in the workday . . . they had expected to go home with empty pockets. They were already bracing to hear the question "Did you work today?" No landlord issues a final-hour invitation, does he?

God does.

No one pays a day's wage to one-hour workers, does he?

God does.

Read Jesus's punch line: "They got the same, each of them

one dollar" (v. 10 MSG). Deathbed converts and lifelong saints enter heaven by the same gate.

Some years ago I took a copy of God's "whoever" policy to California. I wanted to show it to my Uncle Billy. He'd been scheduled to visit my home, but bone cancer had thwarted his plans.

My uncle reminded me much of my father: squared like a blast furnace, ruddy as a leather basketball. They shared the same West Texas roots, penchant for cigars, and blue-collar work ethic. But I wasn't sure if they shared the same faith. So after several planes, two shuttles, and a rental-car road trip, I reached Uncle Billy's house only to learn he was back in the hospital. No visitors. Maybe tomorrow.

He felt better the next day. Good enough to come home. I went to see him. Cancer had taken its toll and his strength. The recliner entombed his body. He recognized me yet dozed as I chatted with his wife and friends. He scarcely opened his eyes. People came and went, and I began to wonder if I would have the chance to ask the question.

Finally the guests stepped out onto the lawn and left me alone with my uncle. I slid my chair next to his, took his skin-taut hand, and wasted no words. "Bill, are you ready to go to heaven?"

His eyes, for the first time, popped open. Saucer wide. His head lifted. Doubt laced his response: "I think I am."

"Do you want to be sure?"

"Oh yes."

Our brief talk ended with a prayer for grace. We both said "amen," and I soon left. Uncle Billy died within days. Did he wake up in heaven? According to the parable of the eleventh-hour workers, he did.

Some struggle with such a thought. A last-minute confessor receives the same grace as a lifetime servant? Doesn't seem fair. The workers in the parable complained too. So the landowner, and God, explained the prerogative of ownership: "Am I not allowed to do what I choose with what belongs to me?" (v. 15 RSV).

Request grace with your dying breath, and God hears your prayer. *Whoever* means "whenever."

And one more: *whoever* means "wherever." *Wherever* you are, you're not too far to come home.

The prodigal son assumed he was. He had spurned his father's kindness and "journeyed to a far country, and there wasted his possessions with prodigal living" (Luke 15:13 NKJV).

The word translated here as *wasted* is the same Greek verb used to describe the action of a seed-sowing farmer. Envision him throwing handfuls of seeds onto tilled earth. Envision the prodigal tossing his father's money to greedy merchants: a roll of bills at one club, a handful of coins at another. He rides the magic carpet of cash from one party to the next.

And then one day his wallet grows thin. The credit card comes back. The maître d' says "no," the hotel says "go," and the boy says "uh-oh." He slides from high hog at the trough to low pig in the mud. He finds employment feeding swine. Not a recommended career path for a Jewish boy.

The hunger so gnaws at his gut he considers eating with the pigs. But rather than swallow the pods, he swallows his pride and begins that famous walk homeward, rehearsing a repentance speech with each step. Turns out he didn't need it. "His father saw him and had compassion, and ran and fell on his neck and kissed him" (v. 20 NKJV). The father was saving the son's place.

He's saving yours too. If heaven's banquet table has name-plates, one bears your name.

We lose much in life—sobriety, solvency, and sanity. We lose jobs and chances, and we lose at love. We lose youth and its vigor, idealism and its dreams. We lose much, but we never lose our place on God's "whoever" list.

Whoever—God's wonderful word of welcome.

I love to hear my wife say "whoever." Sometimes I detect my favorite fragrance wafting from the kitchen: strawberry cake. I follow the smell like a bird dog follows a trail until I'm standing over the just-baked, just-iced pan of pure pleasure. Yet I've learned to still my fork until Denalyn gives clearance.

"Who is it for?" I ask.

She might break my heart. "It's for a birthday party, Max. Don't touch it!"

Or, "For a friend. Stay away."

Or she might throw open the door of delight. "Whoever." And since I qualify as a "whoever," I say "yes."

I so hope you will too. Not to the cake, but to God.

No status too low.

No hour too late.

No place too far.

However. Whenever. Wherever.

Whoever includes you . . . forever.

8

BELIEVE AND RECEIVE

"... whoever believes *in him shall not perish ..."*

Tell me my part again," I groaned.

"Just trust me," she assured. *She* was a bubbly, college-aged, baseball-capped, rope holder. *Trust me* translated into a backward leap off a fifty-foot cliff, wearing a belay harness and a what-did-I-get-myself-into expression.

Some people love rappelling. They relish the stomach-in-the-throat sensation. Not me. I prefer the seat-in-the-chair one. I had traveled to Colorado to experience a week of rest to the fullest. Fresh air, great views. Good coffee, long talks. These events made my list. Half gainers off the mountain didn't.

Blame persuasive friends and stupid pride for my presence on the peak. The platform team assured me of a safe landing.

"Ever done this?" the girl asked.

"No."

She handed me a leather harness and told me to step in. "It's kind of like a diaper." She smiled, all too chipper. *I may need a diaper,* I thought.

"What about you?" I inquired. "Have you lowered anyone down the mountain?"

"Been working here all summer." She beamed.

It was barely July.

"It's simple," she continued as she clipped me in and handed me gloves. "Hold the rope and jump. Bounce off the wall with your feet."

Someone make a law: the words *jump, bounce,* and *wall* should never be spoken in the same breath.

"How do I keep from crashing?"

"You don't. I do that."

"You?"

"Yes, I hold your rope."

Little comfort. Not only was she half my age, she was half my size—more the ballet than the belay sort. "But don't I do *something?*" I begged.

"You trust me."

I inched up to the edge of the cliff and looked down. Frodo felt safer looking into the pit.

"Do you have any valuables?" I heard a voice ask.

"Only my life."

"You're funny," she chirped, sounding so much like my daughters that I remembered my will was out-of-date. "Come on. It's your turn!"

I gave her one more look. A look akin to the one the 3:16 promise often prompts. Can I really trust that "whoever *believes* in him shall not perish"?

Jesus's invitation seems too simple. We gravitate to other

verbs. *Work* has a better ring to it. "Whoever works for him will be saved." *Satisfy* fits nicely. "Whoever satisfies him will be saved." But believe? *Shouldn't I do more?*

This seems to be the struggle of Nicodemus. It was his conversation with Christ, remember, that set the stage for John 3:16. Jesus's "you must be born again" command strikes the scholar—and some of us—the way the words of the take-a-leap girl struck me. What's my part? The baby takes a passive role in the birthing process. The infant allows the parent to do the work. Salvation is equally simple. God works and we trust. Such a thought troubles Nicodemus. *There must be more.* Jesus comforts the visiting professor with an account from the Torah, Nicodemus's favorite book.

> And as Moses lifted up the bronze snake on a pole in the wilderness, so the Son of Man must be lifted up, so that everyone who believes in him will have eternal life. (John 3:14–15 NLT)

Nicodemus knew this event. A one-sentence reference was enough for him to understand the point. The verse is cryptic to us, however. Why did Jesus precede the 3:16 offer with a reference to a serpent in the wilderness? Here is the backstory.

The wandering Israelites were grumbling at Moses again. Though camped on the border of the Promised Land and beneficiaries of four decades of God's provisions, the Hebrews sounded off like spoiled trust-fund brats: "Why have you brought us up out of Egypt to die in the wilderness?" (Num. 21:5 NKJV).

Same complaint, seventieth verse. Ex-slaves longing for Egypt. Dreaming of pyramids and cursing the wasteland, pining for

Pharaoh and vilifying Moses. They hated the hot sand, the long days, and the manna, oh the manna. "Our soul loathes this worthless bread" (v. 5 NKJV).

They'd had all the manna burgers and manna casseroles and manna peanut butter sandwiches they could stomach. And God had had all the moaning he could take. "So the LORD sent fiery serpents among the people, and they bit the people; and many of the people of Israel died" (v. 6 NKJV).

Horror-movie producers long to spawn such scenes. Slithering vipers creep out of holes and rocks and serpentine through the camp. People die. Corpses dot the landscape. Survivors pleaded with Moses to plead with God for mercy. "'We have sinned. . . . Pray to the LORD that He take away the serpents from us.' So Moses prayed for the people. Then the LORD said to Moses, 'Make a fiery serpent, and set it on a pole; and it shall be that everyone who is bitten, when he looks at it, shall live.' So Moses made a bronze serpent, and put it on a pole; and so it was, if a serpent had bitten anyone, when he looked at the bronze serpent, he lived" (vv. 7–9 NKJV).

This passage was a solemn prophecy.

And it was also a simple promise. Snake-bit Israelites found healing by looking at the pole. Sinners will find healing by looking to Christ. "Everyone who believes in him will have eternal life" (John 3:15 NLT).

The simplicity troubles many people. We expect a more complicated cure, a more elaborate treatment. Moses and his followers might have expected more as well. Manufacture an ointment. Invent a therapeutic lotion. Treat one another. Or at least fight back. Break out the sticks and stones and attack the snakes.

We, too, expect a more proactive assignment, to have to conjure up a remedy for our sin. Some mercy seekers have donned hair shirts, climbed cathedral steps on their knees, or traversed hot rocks on bare feet.

Others of us have written our own Bible verse: "God helps those who help themselves" (Popular Opinion 1:1). We'll fix ourselves, thank you. We'll make up for our mistakes with contributions, our guilt with busyness. We'll overcome failures with hard work. We'll find salvation the old-fashioned way: we'll earn it.

Christ, in contrast, says to us what the rope-holding girl said to me: "Your part is to trust. Trust me to do what you can't."

By the way, you take similar steps of trust daily, even hourly. You believe the chair will support you, so you set your weight on it. You believe water will hydrate you, so you swallow it. You trust the work of the light switch, so you flip it. You have faith the doorknob will work, so you turn it.

You regularly trust power you cannot see to do a work you cannot accomplish. Jesus invites you to do the same with him.

Just him. Not Moses or any other leader. Not other snake-bitten souls. Not even you. You can't fix you. Look to Jesus . . . and believe.

Remember my rappelling partner? She told me to fix my gaze on her. As I took the plunge, she shouted, "Keep your eyes up here!" I didn't have to be told twice. She was the only one of the two of us smiling.

But since she did her work, I landed safely. Next trip, however, you'll find me in a chair on the porch.

9

GOD'S GRACIOUS GRIP

*". . . whoever believes in him
shall not perish . . ."*

Team Hoyt consists of a father-son squad: Dick and Rick. They race. They race a lot. Sixty-four marathons. Two hundred and six triathlons. Six triathlons at Ironman distance. Two hundred and four 10K runs. Since 1975, they've crossed nearly a thousand finish lines. They've even crossed the USA. It took them forty-five days to run and pedal 3,735 miles, but they did it.

Team Hoyt loves races. But only half of Team Hoyt can run. Dick, the dad, can. But Rick's legs don't work, nor does his speech. At his birth in 1962, the umbilical cord wrapped around his neck, starving oxygen from his brain, stealing coordination from his body. Doctors gave no hope for his development.

Dick and his wife, Judy, disagreed with the prognosis. Rick couldn't bathe, dress, or feed himself, but he could think. They knew he was bright. So they enrolled him in public school. He graduated. He entered college and graduated again.

But Rick wanted to run. At age fifteen, he asked his dad if they

Cleopatra's Needle stands out like the foreigner she is in London. Her engravings speak of a different era and employ an ancient language. Workers constructed the obelisk 3,500 years ago as a gift for an Egyptian pharaoh. But on September 12, 1878, the British government planted it in English soil and assigned it vigil over the Thames River.

F. W. Boreham was there. He was seven years old the day his father and mother took him on the train to London to witness the moment. He described the "great granite column, smothered with its maze of hieroglyphics." He watched the relic ascend "from the horizontal to the perpendicular, like a giant waking and standing erect after his long, long sleep."

His father explained the significance of the structure: how it once guarded the great temple at Heliopolis. Pharaohs passed it in their chariots. Moses likely studied on its steps. And now, bookended by stone sphinxes, Cleopatra's Needle stood on a British could enter a five-mile benefit race. Dick was not a runner, but he was a father, so he loaded his son in a three-wheeled wheel-chair, and off they went. They haven't stopped since.

Young Rick Hoyt relies on his dad to do it all: lift him, push him, pedal him, and tow him. Other than a willing heart, he makes no contribution to the effort. Rick depends entirely on the strength of his dad.[1]

God wants you to do the same. "Whoever believes *in him* shall not perish but have eternal life" (John 3:16).

The phrase "believes *in him*" doesn't digest well in our day of self-sufficient spiritual food. "Believe *in yourself*" is the common menu selection of our day. Try harder. Work longer. Dig deeper. Self-reliance is our goal.

And tolerance is our virtue. "In him" smacks of exclusion. Don't all paths lead to heaven? Islam, Hinduism, Buddhism, and humanism? Salvation comes in many forms, right? Christ walks upriver on this topic. Salvation is found, not in self or in them, but *in him*.

We bring to the spiritual race what Rick Hoyt brings to the physical one. Our spiritual legs have no strength. Our morality has no muscle. Our good deeds cannot carry us across the finish line, but Christ can. "To the one who does not work, but believes *in Him* who justifies the ungodly, his faith is credited as righteousness" (Rom. 4:5 NASB).

Paul assures salvation to the most unlikely folks: not to the worker, but to the trust-er; not to the able-bodied, but to the unable; not to the affluent saint, but to the bankrupt and un-employable—the child who will trust with Rick Hoyt reliance. "Trusting-him-to-do-it is what gets you set right with God, *by* God. Sheer gift" (Rom. 4:5 MSG).

We bring what Rick brings. And God does what Dick does. He takes start-to-finish-line responsibility for his children. "I give them eternal life, and they shall never perish; no one can snatch them out of my hand" (John 10:28).

Jesus fortified this language with the strongest possible negation, leading the Amplified Bible translators to translate: "And I give them eternal life, and they shall never lose it or perish throughout the ages. [To all eternity they shall never by any means be destroyed.] And no one is able to snatch them out of My hand" (John 10:28).

We parents understand God's resolve. When our children stumble, we do not disown them. When they fall, we do not dismiss them. We may punish or reprimand, but cast them out of the family? We cannot. They are biologically connected to us. Those born with our DNA will die with it.

God, our Father, engenders the same relationship with us. Upon salvation we "become children of God" (John 1:12 ESV). He alters our lineage, redefines our spiritual parenthood, and, in doing so, secures our salvation. To accomplish the mission, he seals us with his Spirit. "Having believed, you were marked in him with a seal, the promised Holy Spirit" (Eph. 1:13). A soul sealed by God is safe.

For a short time in college, I worked at a vacuum-cleaner plant. We assembled the appliance from plug to hose. The last step on the assembly line was "sealing and shipping." By this point, the company had invested hours and dollars in the machine. So they took extra care to protect their product. They mummified it in bubble wrap, secured it with Styrofoam, wrapped the box with tough-to-tear tape, stamped the destination on the box, and belted it inside the truck. That machine was secure. But compared to God's care of his saints, workers dumped bare machines into the back of a pickup truck. God vacuum-seals us with his strongest force: his Spirit. He sheathes his children in a suit of spiritual armor, encircles us with angels, and indwells us himself. The queen of England should enjoy such security.

Christ paid too high a price to leave us unguarded. "Remember, he has identified you as his own, guaranteeing that you will be saved on the day of redemption" (Eph. 4:30 NLT).

What a difference this assurance makes.

An air force pilot told me of the day he forgot to secure himself into the seat of his high-powered jet. He completed every other preliminary act. He satisfied his checklist from beginning to end. Yet he forgot to buckle his seat belt. His jet was configured in such a way that once the plane was airborne, the belt could not be secured. Ejection from the plane meant separation from his seat, and separation from his seat meant separation from his parachute and a face-plant at 120 mph. That'll suck the joy out of the journey. Can you imagine flying a jet without a parachute?

Many do. Eternal insecurity extracts joy from many people. Only Christ guarantees a safe landing. Parallel his offer with that of other religions. Judaism sees salvation as a Judgment Day decision based on morality. Hindus anticipate multiple reincarnations in the soul's journey through the cosmos.[2] Buddhism grades your life according to the Four Noble Truths and the Noble Eightfold Path. Muslims earn their way to Allah by performing the duties of the Five Pillars of Faith.[3] Many philosophers deem life after the grave as hidden and unknown. One called death a step into "the great Perhaps"[4]; another, "a great leap in the dark."[5]

No one but Jesus "buckles you in." You may slip—indeed you will—but you will not fall. Hence the invitation to believe "in him." Don't believe in you; you can't save you. And don't believe in others; they can't save you.

Some historians clump Christ with Moses, Muhammad, Confucius, and other spiritual leaders. But Jesus refuses to share the page. He declares, "I am the way, and the truth, and the life; no one comes to the Father, but by me" (John 14:6 RSV). He could have scored more points in political correctness had he said, "I *know* the way," or "I *show* the way." Yet he speaks not of what he does but of who he is: I *am* the way.

His followers refused to soften or shift the spotlight. Peter announced: "There is salvation in no one else! God has given no other name under heaven by which we must be saved" (Acts 4:12 NLT).

Many recoil at such definitiveness. John 14:6 and Acts 4:12 sound primitive in this era of broadbands and broad minds. The world is shrinking, cultures are blending, borders are bending; this is the day of inclusion. All roads lead to heaven, right?

But can they? The sentence makes good talk-show fodder, but is it accurate? Can all approaches to God be correct?

Islam says Jesus was not crucified. Christians say he was. Both can't be right.

Judaism refuses the claim of Christ as the Messiah.[6] Christians accept it. Someone's making a mistake.

Buddhists look toward Nirvana, achieved after no less than 547 reincarnations.[7] Christians believe in one life, one death, and an eternity of enjoying God. Doesn't one view exclude the other?

Humanists do not acknowledge a creator of life. Jesus claims to be the source of life. One of the two speaks folly.

Spiritists read your palms. Christians consult the Bible.

Hindus perceive a plural and impersonal God.[8] Christ-follow-ers believe "there is only one God" (1 Cor. 8:4 NLT). Somebody is wrong.

And, most supremely, every non-Christian religion says, "You can save you." Jesus says, "My death on the cross saves you."

How can all religions lead to God when they are so different? We don't tolerate such illogic in other matters. We don't pretend that all roads lead to London or all ships sail to Australia. All flights don't land in Rome. Imagine your response to a travel agent who claims they do. You tell him you need a flight to Rome, Italy, so he looks on his screen.

"Well, there is a flight to Sydney, Australia, departing at 6:00 a.m."

"Does it go to Rome?"

"No, but it offers wonderful in-flight dining and movies."

"But I need to go to Rome."

"Then let me suggest Southwest Airlines."

"Southwest Airlines flies to Rome?"

"No, but they have consistently won awards for on-time arrivals."

You're growing frustrated. "I need one airline to carry me to one place: Rome."

The agent appears offended. "Sir, all flights go to Rome."

You know better. Different flights have different destinations. That's not a thickheaded conclusion but an honest one. Every flight does not go to Rome. Every path does not lead to God. Jesus blazed a stand-alone trail void of self-salvation. He cleared a one-of-a-kind passageway uncluttered by human effort. Christ came, not for the strong, but for the weak; not for the righteous, but for the sinner. We enter his way upon confession of our need, not completion of our deeds. He offers a unique-to-him invitation in which he works and we trust, he dies and we live, he invites and we believe.

We believe *in him*. "The work God wants you to do is this: Believe the One he sent" (John 6:29 NCV).

Believe in yourself? No. Believe in him.

Believe in them? No. Believe in him.

And those who do, those who believe "in him shall not perish but have eternal life" (John 3:16).

How do we begin to believe? We do what young Rick Hoyt did. We turn to our Father for help.

When Dick and Rick Hoyt cross finish lines, both receive finisher medals. Post-race listings include both names. The dad does the work, but the son shares in the victory. Why? Because he believes. And because he believes, both celebrate the finish.

May you and your Father do the same.

10

HELL'S SUPREME SURPRISE

*". . . whoever believes in him
shall not perish . . ."*

The hero of heaven is God. Angels don't worship mansions or glittering avenues. Neither gates nor jewels prompt the hosts to sing . . . God does. His majesty stirs the pen of heaven's poets and the awe of her citizens.

They enjoy an eternity-long answer to David's prayer: "One thing I ask of the LORD . . . to gaze upon the beauty of the LORD" (Ps. 27:4). What else warrants a look? Inhabitants of heaven forever marvel at the sins God forgives, the promises he keeps, the plan he executes. He's not the grand marshal of the parade; he is the parade. He's not the main event; he's the only event. His Broadway features a single stage and star: himself. He hosts the only production and invites every living soul to attend.

He, at this very moment, issues invitations by the millions. He whispers through the kindness of a grandparent, shouts through the tempest of a tsunami. Through the funeral he cautions, "Life is fragile." Through a sickness he reminds, "Days are numbered."

God may speak through nature or nurture, majesty or mishap. But through all and to all he invites: "Come, enjoy me forever."

Yet many people have no desire to do so. They don't want anything to do with God. He speaks; they cover their ears. He commands; they scoff. They don't want him telling them how to live. They mock what he says about marriage, money, sex, or the value of human life. They regard his son as a joke and the cross as utter folly.[1] They spend their lives telling God to leave them alone. And at the moment of their final breath, he honors their request: "Get away from me, you who do evil. I never knew you" (Matt. 7:23 NCV). This verse escorts us to the most somber of Christian realities: hell.

No topic stirs greater resistance. Who wants to think about eternal punishment? We prefer to casualize the issue, making jokes about its residents or turning the noun into a flippant adjective. "That was a hell of a steak." Odd that we don't do the same with lesser tragedies. You never hear, "My golf game has gone to *prison*." Or, "This is an AIDS of a traffic jam." Seems a conspiracy is afoot to minimize hell.

Some prefer to sanitize the subject, dismissing it as a moral impossibility.

"I do not myself feel that any person," defied atheist Bertrand Russell, "who is really profoundly humane can believe in everlasting punishment."[2] Or, as is more commonly believed, "A loving God would not send people to hell." Religious leaders increasingly agree. Martin Marty, a church historian at the University of Chicago Divinity School, canvassed one hundred years of some scholarly journals for entries on hell. He didn't find one. "Hell," he observed, "disappeared and no one noticed."[3]

Easy to understand why. Hell is a hideous topic. Any person

who discusses it glibly or proclaims it gleefully has failed to ponder it deeply. Scripture writers dip pens in gloomy ink to describe its nature. They speak of the "blackest darkness" (Jude 13), "everlasting destruction" (2 Thess. 1:9), "weeping and gnashing of teeth" (Matt. 8:12).

A glimpse into the pit won't brighten your day, but it will enlighten your understanding of Jesus. He didn't avoid the discussion. Quite the contrary. He planted a one-word caution sign between you and hell's path: *perish.* "Whoever believes in him shall not *perish* but have eternal life" (John 3:16).

Jesus spoke of hell often. Thirteen percent of his teachings refer to eternal judgment and hell.[4] Two-thirds of his parables relate to resurrection and judgment.[5] Jesus wasn't cruel or capricious, but he was blunt. His candor stuns.

He speaks in tangible terms. "Fear Him," he warns, "who is able to destroy both soul and body in hell" (Matt. 10:28 NKJV). He quotes Hades's rich man pleading for Lazarus to "dip the tip of his finger in water and cool my tongue" (Luke 16:24 NKJV). Words such as *body, finger,* and *tongue* presuppose a physical state in which a throat longs for water and a person begs for relief—physical relief.

The apostles said that Judas Iscariot had gone "to his own place" (Acts 1:25 NASB). The Greek word for place is *topos,* which means geographical location.[6] Jesus describes heaven with the same noun: "In My Father's house are many mansions. . . . I go to prepare a place for you" (John 14:2 NKJV). Hell, like heaven, is a location, not a state of mind, not a metaphysical dimension of floating spirits, but an actual place populated by physical beings.

Woeful, this thought. God has quarantined a precinct in his vast universe as the depository of the hard-hearted.

Exactly where is hell? Jesus gives one chilling clue: "outside." "Tie him hand and foot, and throw him *outside*, into the darkness" (Matt. 22:13). Outside of what? Outside of the boundaries of heaven, for one thing. Abraham, in paradise, told the rich man, in torment, "Between us and you there is a great gulf fixed, so that those who want to pass from here to you cannot, nor can those from there pass to us" (Luke 16:26 NKJV). No heaven-to-hell field trips. No hell-to-heaven holiday breaks. Hell is to heaven what the edge of our universe is to earth: outside the range of a commute.

Hell is also outside the realm of conclusion. Oh, that hell's punishment would end, that God would schedule an execution date. New Testament language leads some godly scholars to believe he will:

Fear Him who is able to *destroy* both soul and body in hell. (Matt. 10:28 NKJV)

Whoever believes in him shall not *perish*. (John 3:16)

Destroy. Perish. Don't such words imply an end to suffering? I wish I could say they do. There is no point on which I'd more gladly be wrong than the eternal duration of hell. If God, on the last day, extinguishes the wicked, I'll celebrate my misreading of his words. Yet annihilation seems inconsistent with Scripture. God sobers his warnings with eternal language. Consider John's description of the wicked in Revelation 14:11: "the smoke of their torment goes up forever and ever, and they have no rest, day or night" (ESV). How could the euthanized soul "have no rest, day or night"?

Jesus parallels hell with Gehenna, a rubbish dump outside the southwestern walls of Jerusalem, infamous for its unending smoldering and decay. He employs Gehenna as a word picture of hell, the place where the "worm does not die and the fire is not quenched" (Mark 9:48 ESV). A deathless worm and quenchless fire—however symbolic these phrases may be—smack of ongoing consumption of something. Jesus speaks of sinners being "thrown outside, into the darkness, where there will be weeping and gnashing of teeth" (Matt. 8:12). How can a nonexistent person weep or gnash teeth?

Jesus describes the length of heaven and hell with the same adjective: *eternal*. "They will go away into eternal punishment, but the righteous into eternal life" (Matt. 25:46 RSV). Hell lasts as long as heaven. It may have a back door or graduation day, but I haven't found it.

Much perishes in hell. Hope perishes. Happiness perishes. But the body and soul of the God-deniers continue outside. Outside of heaven, outside of hope, and outside of God's goodness.

None of us have seen such a blessingless world. Even the vilest precincts of humanity know the grace of God. People who want nothing of God still enjoy his benefits. Adolf Hitler witnessed the wonder of the Alps. Saddam Hussein enjoyed the blushing sunrise of the desert. The dictator, child molester, serial rapist, and drug peddler—all enjoy the common grace of God's goodness. They hear children laugh, smell dinner cooking, and tap their toes to the rhythm of a good song. They deny God yet enjoy his benevolence.

But these privileges are confiscated at the gateway to hell. Scofflaws will be "shut out from the presence of the Lord" (2 Thess. 1:9). Hell knows none of heaven's kindnesses, no overflow of divine perks. The only laughter the unrepentant hear is evil; the only desires they know are selfish. As the Scottish professor James Denney describes it, God-rejecters "pass into a night on which no morning dawns."[7] Hell is society at its worst.

More tragically, hell is individuals at their worst. It surfaces and amplifies the ugliest traits in people. Cravings will go unchecked. Worriers will fret and never find peace. Thieves will steal and never have enough. Drunks always craving, gluttons always demanding. None will be satisfied. Remember: "their worm does not die" (Mark 9:48 ESV). As one writer put it, "Not only will the unbeliever be in hell, but hell will be in him too."[8]

Death freezes the moral compass. People will remain in the fashion they enter. Revelation 22:11 seems to emphasize hell's unrepentant evil: "Let the evildoer still do evil, and the filthy still be filthy" (RSV). The God-less remain ungodly.

Hell is not a correctional facility or reform school. Its members hear no admonishing parents, candid sermons, or Spirit of God, no voice of God, no voice of God's people. Spend a lifetime telling God to be quiet, and he'll do just that. God honors our request for silence.

Hell is the chosen home of insurrectionists, the Alcatraz of malcontents. Hell is reserved, not for those souls who seek God yet struggle, but for those who defy God and rebel. For those who say about Jesus, "We don't want this man to be our king" (Luke 19:14). So in history's highest expression of fairness, God honors their preference. "I take no pleasure in the death of the wicked, but rather that they turn from their ways and live" (Ezek. 33:11). It is not his will that any should perish, but the fact that some do highlights God's justice. God must punish sin. "Nothing impure will ever enter [heaven], nor will anyone who does what is shameful or deceitful, but only those whose names are written in the Lamb's book of life" (Rev. 21:27). God, inherently holy, *must* exclude evil from his new universe. God, eternally gracious, *never* forces his will. He urges mutineers to stay on board but never ties them to the mast. C. S. Lewis wrote, "I willingly believe that the damned are, in one sense, successful rebels to the end; that the doors of hell are locked on the inside."[9] How could a loving God send sinners to hell? He doesn't. They volunteer.

Once there, they don't want to leave. The hearts of damned fools never soften; their minds never change. "Men were scorched with great heat, and they blasphemed the name of God who has power over these plagues; and they did not repent and give Him glory" (Rev. 16:9 NKJV). Contrary to the idea that hell prompts remorse, it doesn't. It intensifies blasphemy.

Remember the rich man in torment? He could see heaven but didn't request a transfer. He wanted Lazarus to descend to him. Why not ask if he could join Lazarus? The rich man complained of thirst, not of injustice. He wanted water for the body, not water for the soul. Even the longing for God is a gift from God, and where there is no more of God's goodness, there is no longing for him. Though every knee shall bow before God and every tongue confess his preeminence (Rom. 14:11), the hard-hearted will do so stubbornly and without worship. There will be no atheists in hell (Phil. 2:10–11), but there will be no God-seekers either.

But still we wonder, is the punishment fair? Such a penalty seems inconsistent with a God of love—overkill. A sinner's rebellion doesn't warrant an eternity of suffering, does it? Isn't God overreacting?

A man once accused me of the same. Some years ago, when

my daughters were small, we encountered an impatient shopper at a convenience store. My three girls were selecting pastries from the doughnut shelf. They weren't moving quickly enough for him, so he leaned over their shoulders and barked, "You kids hurry up. You're taking too long." I, an aisle away, overheard the derision and approached him. "Sir, those are my daughters. They didn't deserve those words. You need to apologize to them."

He minimized the offense. "I didn't do anything that bad."

My response? That verdict was not his to render. Those were my daughters he had hurt. Who was he to challenge my reaction? Who are we to challenge God's? Only he knows the full story, the number of invitations the stubborn-hearted have refused and the slander they've spewed.

Accuse God of unfairness? He has wrapped caution tape on hell's porch and posted a million and one red flags outside the entrance. To descend its stairs, you'd have to cover your ears, blindfold your eyes, and, most of all, ignore the epic sacrifice of history: Christ, in God's hell on humanity's cross, crying out to the blackened sky, "My God, my God, why have you forsaken me?" (Matt. 27:46). You'll more easily capture the Pacific in a jar than describe that sacrifice in words. But a description might read like this: God, who hates sin, unleashed his wrath on his sin-filled son. Christ, who never sinned, endured the awful forsakenness of hell. The supreme surprise of hell is this: Christ went there so you won't have to. Yet hell could not contain him. He arose, not just from the dead, but from the depths. "Through death He [destroyed] him who had the power of death, that is, the devil" (Heb. 2:14 NKJV).

Christ emerged from Satan's domain with this declaration: "I have the keys of Hades and of Death" (Rev. 1:18 NKJV). He is the warden of eternity. The door he shuts, no one opens. The door he opens, no one shuts (Rev. 3:7).

Thanks to Christ, this earth can be the nearest you come to hell.

But apart from Christ, this earth is the nearest you'll come to heaven.

A friend told me about the final hours of her aunt. The woman lived her life with no fear of God or respect for his Word. She was an atheist. Even in her final days, she refused to permit anyone to speak of God or eternity. Only her Maker knows her last thoughts and eternal destiny, but her family heard her final words. Hours from death, scarcely conscious of her surroundings, she opened her eyes. Addressing a face visible only to her, she defied, "You don't know me? You don't know me?"

Was she hearing the pronouncement of Christ: "I never knew you; depart from me" (Matt. 7:23 ESV)?

Contrast her words with those of a Christ-follower. The dying man made no secret of his faith or longing for heaven. Two days before he succumbed to cancer, he awoke from a deep sleep and told his wife, "I'm living in two realities. I'm not allowed to tell you. There are others in this room." And on the day he died, he opened his eyes and asked, "Am I special? Why, that I should be allowed to see all this?"

Facing death with fear or faith, dread or joy. "Whoever believes in him shall not perish . . ." God makes the offer. We make the choice.

11

WHAT MAKES HEAVEN HEAVENLY

". . . shall not perish but have eternal life"

In one of his *Far Side* cartoons, Gary Larson depicts a winged man seated in heaven on a cloud. No one near. Nothing to do. Marooned on his celestial post. The caption witnesses his despair: "Wish I'd brought a magazine."[1]

We can relate. *Eternal* life? Clouds in our midst, harps on our laps, and time on our hands, unending time. Forever and ever. Nonstop. An endless sing-along. A hymn, then a chorus, then still more verses. Hmm . . . that's it? "Whatever the tortures of hell," declared Isaac Asimov, "I think the boredom of heaven would be even worse."[2]

You might have similar reservations. Quiet, yet troubling ones. Will eternity meet expectations? Can heaven deliver on its promises? Jesus gives an assuring response to such questions:

Don't let your hearts be troubled. Trust in God, and trust also in me. There is more than enough room in my Father's home.

If this were not so, would I have told you that I am going to
prepare a place for you? When everything is ready, I will come
and get you, so that you will always be with me where I am.
(John 14:1–3 NLT)

The movies have told you wrong. Those images of knee-high
fog banks, disembodied friends, and floating spirits? Forget
them. Jesus has gone to "prepare a *place*." Like hell, heaven is
tangible and touchable: as real as the soil in your garden, as physical as the fruit in your orchard. In fact, your garden and fruit
might look familiar in heaven.

We assume God will destroy this universe and relocate his
children . . . but why would he? When God created the heavens
and earth, he applauded his work. God saw:

The light . . . it was good.
The sea . . . it was good.
The grass . . . it was good.
The sun . . . the moon . . . it was good (Gen. 1).

Straight-A report card. One perfect score followed another.
"God saw everything that He had made, and indeed it was very
good" (v. 31 NKJV).

Why obliterate a work of art? God never denounced his earth,
just our mistreatment of it. Besides, he is the God of reclamation,
not extermination. He restores, recovers, renews. Expect and
look for him to do it again—to renew and reclaim every square
inch of what is rightfully his. "In the *re-creation* of the world,
when the Son of Man will rule gloriously, you who have followed
me will also rule" (Matt. 19:28 MSG).

But what about the promises of the earth's destruction? Peter and John use A-bomb terminology. "Disappear with a roar . . . destroyed by fire . . . laid bare . . . passed away" (2 Pet. 3:10; Rev. 21:1). Won't this planet be destroyed? Yes, but destruction need not mean elimination. Our bodies provide a prototype. They will pass away, return to dust. Yet the one who called Adam out of a dirt pile will do so with us. Christ will reverse decomposition with resurrection. Amino acids will regenerate. Lungs will awaken. Molecules will reconnect. The mortal body will put on immortality (1 Cor. 15:53).

The same is true about earth. Paul says that the "whole creation groans and suffers the pains of childbirth together until now" (Rom. 8:22 NASB). Like a mother in labor, nature looks toward her delivery day. We see the birth pangs: floods, volcanoes, earthquakes. We contribute to them: polluting the sky, pillaging the soil. God's creation struggles, but not forever. He will purge, cleanse, and reconstruct his cosmos. In the renewal of all things, pristine purity will flow, as Eden promised.

God grants glimpses of this future state. He designed an oculus in this pantheon. Through it we see gold-drenched sunsets. Diamond-studded night skies. Rainbows so arched in splendor we have to stop and sigh. Appetizers of heaven.

But nothing compares with God's crowning jewel: the New Jerusalem. Christ will descend in a city unlike any the earth has ever seen. "I, John, saw the holy city, New Jerusalem, coming" (Rev. 21:2 NKJV). Scripture reveals its jaw-dropping dimensions: an exact square of 1,400 miles (v. 16). Large enough to contain all the land mass from the Appalachians to the California coast—Canada to Mexico. Forty times the size of England, ten times the size of France, and larger than India. And that's just the ground floor.

The city stands as tall as it does wide. Supposing God stacks floors in his metropolis as an architect would in a building, the city would have over 600,000 stories, ample space for billions of people to come and go.

Come and go they will. The gates are never closed (v. 25). Why shut them? The enemies of God will be banished! The wicked will be quarantined, leaving only a perfect place of perfected people.

You will be you at your best forever. Even now you have your good moments. Occasional glimpses of your heavenly self. When you change your baby's diaper, forgive your boss's temper, tolerate your spouse's moodiness, you display traces of saintliness. It's the other moments that sour life. Tongue, sharp as a razor. Moods as unpredictable as Mount Saint Helens. This part wearies you.

But God impounds imperfections at his gate. His light silences the wolfman within. "Nothing that is impure will enter the city" (v. 27 TEV). Pause and let this promise drench you. Can you envision your sinless existence?

Just think what Satan has taken from you, even in the last few hours. You worried about a decision and envied someone's success, dreaded a conversation and resented an interruption. He's been prowling your environs all day, pickpocketing peace, joy, belly laughs, and honest love. Rotten freebooter.

But his days are numbered. Unlike he did in the Garden of Eden, Satan will not lurk in heaven's gardens. "There shall be no more curse" (22:3 NKJV). He will not tempt; hence, you will not stumble. "The world is passing away, and *the lust of it;* but he who does the will of God abides forever" (1 John 2:17 NKJV).

You will be you at your best forever!

And you'll enjoy everyone else at their prime! As it is, one of us is always a step behind. Bad moods infect the best of families. Complaints shadow the clearest days. Bad apples spoil bunches of us, but rotten fruit doesn't qualify for the produce section of heaven. Christ will have completed his redemptive work. All gossip excised and jealousy extracted. He will suction the last drop of orneriness from the most remote corners of our souls. You'll love the result. No one will doubt your word, question your motives, or speak evil behind your back. God's sin purging discontinues all strife.

Dare we imagine heaven's dramatic reunions?

- A soldier embracing the sharpshooter who killed him
- A daughter seeing her abusive but repentant father and holding him
- A son encountering the mother who aborted him? No doubt some will. And when they do, forgiveness will flow like water over Iguaça Falls.

"The wolf will live with the lamb" (Isa. 11:6). "God will wipe away every tear . . . there shall be no more death, nor sorrow, nor crying . . . for the former things have passed away" (Rev. 21:4 NKJV).

No sin means no thieves, divorce, heartbreak, and no boredom. You won't be bored in heaven, because you won't be the same *you* in heaven. Boredom emerges from soils that heaven disallows. The soil of weariness: our eyes tire. Mental limitations: information overload dulls us. Self-centeredness: we grow disinterested when the spotlight shifts to others. Tedium: meaningless activity siphons vigor.

But Satan will take these weedy soils to hell with him, leaving you with a keen mind, endless focus, and God-honoring assignments.

Yes, you will have assignments in heaven. God gave Adam and Eve garden responsibilities. "Let them have dominion" (Gen. 1:26 NKJV). He mantled the couple with leadership over "the fish of the sea, over the birds of the air, and over the cattle, over all the earth and over every creeping thing that creeps on the earth" (v. 26 NKJV). Adam was placed in the garden "to tend and keep it" (2:15 NKJV).

Adam and his descendants will do it again. "[God's] servants shall serve Him" (Rev. 22:3 NKJV). What is service if not responsible activity? Those who are faithful over a few things will rule over many (Matt. 25:21).

You might oversee the orbit of a distant planetary system . . . design a mural in the new city . . . monitor the expansion of a new species of plants or animals. "Of the increase of His government and peace there will be no end" (Isa. 9:7 NKJV). God's new world will be marked by increase. Increased planets? Colors? Music? Seems likely. What does a creator do but create?

What do his happy children do but serve him? We might serve in the capacity we serve now. Couldn't earthly assignments hint at heavenly ones? Architects of Moscow might draw blueprints in the new Liverpool. We will feast in heaven; you may be a cook on Saturn. God filled his first garden with plants and animals. He'll surely do the same in heaven. If so, he may entrust you with the care and feeding of an Africa or two.

One thing is for sure: you'll love it. Never weary, selfish, or defeated. Clear mind, tireless muscles, unhindered joy. Heaven is a perfect place of perfected people with our perfect Lord. "Oh, the depth of the riches both of the wisdom and knowledge of God! How unsearchable are His judgments and His ways past finding out!" (Rom. 11:33 NKJV).

Don't assume we will exhaust our study of God. Endless attributes await us. His grace will increasingly stun, wisdom progressively astound, and perfection ever more sharpen into focus.

We serve a God so rapt with wonders that their viewing requires an eternity. A God whose beauty enhances with proximity. And this is the invitation he gives: "When everything is ready, I will come and get you, so that you will always be with me where I am" (John 14:3 NLT).

John Todd was very young when the deaths of his parents left him orphaned. He was one of several children, and, as was common in the early 1800s, he and all his siblings were farmed out to relatives. An aunt offered to take little John. She sent a servant by the name of Caesar to bring John to her. The boy climbed on the back of the horse, wrapped his small arms around the man, and set out for her house. His questions unveiled his fears.

"Will she be there?"

"Oh, yes," Caesar assured. "She'll be there waiting up for you."

"Will I like living with her?"

"My son, you fall into good hands."

"Will she love me?"

The servant was patient and soft in his reply. "Ah, she has a big heart."

"Do you think she'll go to bed before we get there?"

"Oh, no! She'll be sure to wait up for you. You'll see when we get out of these woods. You'll see her candle in the window."

Sure enough, as they neared the house, John saw a candle in the window and his aunt standing in the doorway. As he shyly approached the porch, she reached down and kissed him and said, "Welcome home!"

Young John Todd grew up in his aunt's care. She was a mother to him. When the time came for him to select a profession, he followed a calling into the pastorate. Years later, the role with his aunt was reversed. She sent news of her failing health and impending death. Here is what he wrote in reply:

> My Dear Aunt,
> Years ago, I left a house of death, not knowing where I was to go, whether anyone cared, whether it was the end of me. The ride was long, but the servant encouraged me. Finally I arrived to your embrace and a new home. I was expected; I felt safe. You did it all for me.
>
> Now it's your turn to go. I'm writing to let you know, someone is waiting up, your room is all ready, the light is on, the door is open, and you're expected![3]

As are you. Jesus is preparing for you a place. A perfect place of perfected people overseen by our perfect Lord. And at the right time he will come and take you home.

12

THE LAST WORD
ON LIFE

". . . shall not perish but have eternal life"

A friend from my West Texas hometown contacted me with some big news. "My father saw your mother's name in an unclaimed property column of the local newspaper."

I couldn't imagine what the property might be. Dad died years ago. Mom lives near my sister in Arkansas. We sold her house. As far as I knew, we owned nothing in the city. "Unclaimed property?"

"Sure, city hall is obliged to list the names of folks who own these goods."

"You don't say."

"I'll send you the contact information."

That was on Sunday. His e-mail arrived on Tuesday. That left me the better part of forty-eight hours to imagine what my folks, unbeknownst to their kids, had hoarded away. Initially, I was stumped. The Great Depression honed my parents into penny-pinchers. They did to dollars what boa constrictors do to rats—squeezed the life out of them.

Then again, Dad worked as an oil-field mechanic. Wildcatters roam such parts. Did one convince him to quietly invest a few bucks in a long-shot oil well? Did he keep it from Mom lest she erupt? And now, could it be that the well has oil? A petroleum gusher might mean millions, no, zillions of barrels of black gold flowing from the Devonian treasure. And who is listed among the investors but Jack Lucado. And who is listed among his heirs?

My imagination raced like a Formula One driver. *This could be big.* By Sunday evening I'd funded my yet-to-be-born grand-children's education. On Monday I ended world hunger. Tuesday, as the e-mail came, I was solving the AIDS crisis. I dialed the courthouse number. The clerk remembered my mom and, with no small enthusiasm, affirmed, "I've been hoping you'd call." I heard papers shuffling, her voice mumbling, "Now where did I put that check?"

Check? Gulp. I pulled a calculator out of my desk and lim-bered my fingers. "Here it is!" she exclaimed, speaking back into the phone. "Looks like we owe your mom some money. Whoa, this has been here awhile."

I drummed my fingers on the desk.

"Let's see, Mr. Lucado. Where should we send this check?"

I gave her an address and waited.

She continued. "Looks like we owe your mom three fifty."

Did she say th-th-three hundred and fifty million? I collected myself. She might mean thousand. *Whichever, way to go, Dad.*

"Yes, sir, your mother overpaid her final water bill by three dollars and fifty cents. Shall I send that today?"

"Sure . . . thanks. Just put it in the mail."

Some hopes fail to deliver. Some expectations sputter and flop like an untied balloon. Remember the shining-armor boyfriend who became the heartbreaking two-timer? The fast-track promotion that landed you in the forgotten basement cubicle? The cross-country move you made to "find yourself"? You found yourself, all right. You found yourself with higher rent and fewer friends.

"If only" dreams lurk in each biography. "If only I could find a mate . . . a career . . . a bright red, affordable '65 Mustang." The only barrier between you and bliss is an "if only." Sometimes you cross it. You find the mate or the career or the Mustang and . . . you count the three fifty and sigh.

Life has letdowns. And how do you know Christ won't be one of them? Honestly. Dare you believe that he gives what he promises to give? Life. Eternal life. "Whoever believes in him shall not perish but have eternal life" (John 3:16). We're pulling into the final station. Having worked our way through the 3:16 itinerary, we need to ponder one more word: *life.*

Beer companies offer you life in their hops. Perfume makers promise new life for your romance. But don't confuse costume jewelry with God's sapphire.

Jesus offers *zoe,* the Greek word for "life as God has it."[1] Whereas *bios,* its sibling term, is life extensive, *zoe* is life intensive. Jesus talks less about life's duration and more about its quality, vitality, energy, and fulfillment. What the new mate, sports car, or unexpected check could never do, Christ says, "I can." You'll love how he achieves it. He reconnects your soul with God.

What God gave Adam and Eve, he entrusted to you and me. A soul. "The LORD God formed man of the dust of the ground, and breathed into his nostrils the breath of life; and man became a living being" (Gen. 2:7 NKJV).

You, a bipedal ape? Chemical fluke? Atomic surprise? By no

means. You bear the very breath of God. He exhaled himself into you, making you a "living being" (v. 7).

The Hebrew word translated here as "being" is *nephesh*, which appears over 750 times in the Bible. It sometimes refers to the life force present in all creatures. In the context of a person, however, *nephesh* refers to our souls.[2]

Your soul distinguishes you from zoo dwellers. God gifted the camel with a hump and the giraffe with a flagpole neck, but he reserved his breath, or a soul, for you. You bear his stamp. You do things God does. Think. Question. Reflect. You blueprint buildings, chart sea crossings, and swallow throat lumps when your kids say their alphabet. You, like Adam, have a soul.

And, like Adam, you've used your soul to disobey God. God's command to the charter couple includes the Bible's first reference to death. "You must not eat from the tree of the knowledge of good and evil, for when you eat of it you will surely die" (v. 17).

My daughter Andrea, when elementary-school age, asked a grown-up question. "Dad, if God didn't want them to eat from the tree, why did he put it there?" The answer, best I can tell, is to remind us who created whom. When we attempt to swap roles with God and tell him we can eat (think, say, do, control, own, hurt, inhale, ingest, demand) anything we want, we die two deaths. Adam and Eve did. They died physically, eventually, and spiritually, instantly.

Reread God's warning: "*when* you eat of it you will surely die" (v. 17). Sin resulted in Adam's and Eve's immediate deaths. But death of what? Their bodies? No, they continued to breathe. Brain waves flowed. Eyelids blinked. Their bodies functioned, but their hearts hardened. They stopped trusting God. Their friendship with their maker died.

We understand how this happened. If you loan me your car and I wreck it, will I want to see you again? No. I will dread our next encounter. Adam and Eve experienced the same.

Prior to this act, they followed God like sheep follow their shepherd. He spoke; they listened. He gave assignments; they fulfilled them. They were naked but unashamed, transparent and unafraid. Yet as one drop of ink clouds a glass of water, the stubborn deed darkened their souls. Everything changed. God's presence stirred panic, not peace. Adam ran like a kid caught raiding the pantry. "I was afraid" (Gen. 3:10). Intimacy with God ceased; separation from God began. We'll always wonder why Adam didn't ask for forgiveness. But he didn't, and the guilty pair was "banished . . . from the Garden of Eden" (Gen. 3:23).

We've loitered outside the gates ever since.

Deep within we've known (haven't we known?) something is awry—we feel disconnected. What we hope will bring life brings limited amounts . . . three fifty worth. We connect with a career, find meaning in family, yet long for something more.

We feel the frustration I felt on Christmas morning, 1964. I assembled a nine-year-old's dream gift: a genuine Santa Fe Railroad miniature train set, complete with battery-powered engine and flashing crossing lights. I placed the locomotive on the tracks and watched in sheer glee as three pounds of pure steel wound its way across my bedroom floor. Around and around and around and . . . around . . . and around . . . After some time I picked it up and turned it the other direction. It went around and around and around . . .

"Mom, what else did you get me for Christmas?"

Similarly, our lives chug in long ovals, one lap after another.

First job. Promotion. Wedding day. Nursery beds. Kids. Grandkids. Around and around . . . Is there anything else?

Our dissatisfaction mates with disappointment and gives birth to some unruly children: drunkenness, power plays, eighty-hour workweeks, nosedives into sexual perversions—all nothing more than poorly disguised longings for Eden. We long to restore what Adam lost. As someone once said, "The man who knocks on the door of a brothel is seeking God."

Where and when the brothel fails, Jesus steps forth with a reconnection invitation. Though we be "dead in [our] transgressions and sins[3] and separated from the life of God,[4] whoever believes that Jesus is the Christ is born of God.[5] Reborn! This is not a physical birth resulting from human passion or plan—this rebirth comes from God."[6]

Don't miss the invisible, inward miracle triggered by belief. God reinstates us to Garden-of-Eden status. What Adam and Eve did, we now do! The flagship family walked with God; we can too. They heard his voice; so can we. They were naked and unashamed; we can be transparent and unafraid. No more running or hiding.

He breathes life into flatlined lives. He does for our hearts what we do for dead car batteries. I had one recently. I turned my ignition—no noise. So I did what anyone would do: I doused my car with a fifth of whiskey, confident that a bottle of eighty proof would stir some life. Nothing happened. I rolled a television in front of the grill and flipped on the game. A good contest perks up the deadest cell, right? Not this time. So I purchased the latest issue of *Pent-Garage* and let my automobile feast her headlights on some European beauties. No response. The battery had the punch of a shoe box.

And you think I have the IQ of a screwdriver. Who turns to booze, screens, or bodies for renewal? Too many. Far too many.

But Jesus's offer still stands. "Because Jesus was raised from the dead, we've been given a brand-new life and have everything to live for, including a future in heaven—and the future starts now!" (1 Pet. 1:3–4 MSG).

Others offer life, but no one offers to do what Jesus does—to reconnect us to his power. But how can we know? How do we know that Jesus knows what he's talking about? The ultimate answer, according to his flagship followers, is the vacated tomb. Did you note the words you just read? "Because Jesus was *raised from the dead,* we've been given a brand-new life." In the final sum, it was the disrupted grave that convinced the maiden Christians to cast their lots with Christ. "He was seen by Peter and then by the twelve apostles. After that, Jesus was seen by more than five hundred of the believers at the same time" (1 Cor. 15:5–6 NCV).

Can Jesus actually replace death with life? He did a convincing job with his own. We can trust him because he has been there.

On a trip to China, I rode past Tiananmen Square in a bus full of Westerners. We tried to recollect the causes and consequences of the revolt. Our knowledge of history was embarrassing. One gave one date; another gave a different one. One person remembered a certain death toll; someone else disagreed. All this time our translator remained silent.

Finally one of us asked her, "Do you remember anything about the Tiananmen Square revolt?"

Her answer was solemn. "Yes, I was a part of it."

We quickly grew quiet as she gave firsthand recollections of the bloodshed and oppression. We listened, because she'd been there.

We who follow Christ do so for the same reason. He's been there . . .

He's been to Bethlehem, wearing barn rags and hearing sheep crunch. Suckling milk and shivering against the cold. All of divinity content to cocoon itself in an eight-pound body and to sleep on a cow's supper. Millions who face the chill of empty pockets or the fears of sudden change turn to Christ. Why?

Because he's been there.

He's been to Nazareth, where he made deadlines and paid bills; to Galilee, where he recruited direct reports and separated fighters; to Jerusalem, where he stared down critics and stood up against cynics.

We have our Nazareths as well—demands and due dates. Jesus wasn't the last to build a team; accusers didn't disappear with Jerusalem's temple. Why seek Jesus's help with your challenges? Because he's been there. To Nazareth, to Galilee, to Jerusalem.

But most of all, he's been to the grave. Not as a visitor, but as a corpse. Buried amidst the cadavers. Numbered among the dead. Heart silent and lungs vacant. Body wrapped and grave sealed. The cemetery. He's been buried there.

You haven't yet. But you will be. And since you will, don't you need someone who knows the way out?

God . . . has given us new birth into a living hope through the resurrection of Jesus Christ from the dead. . . . He destroyed death, and through the Good News he showed us the way to have life that cannot be destroyed. (1 Pet. 1:3 NIV; 2 Tim. 1:10 NCV)

Remember that check from my hometown? I'm still waiting on it. Not counting on it for much. The three fifty promises to bring little. But the 3:16 promise? I've long since deposited that check. It bears interest every day and will forever.

Yours will too.

CONCLUSION

THE 3:16ED LIFE

F ree flight: Rio de Janeiro to Miami, Florida."
I wasn't the only person to hear about the offer but one of
the few to phone and request details. The courier service offered
an airline ticket to anyone willing to carry a bag of mail to the
States. The deal was tantalizingly simple:

> Meet the company representative at the airport, where you'll be
> given a duffel bag of documents and one ticket. Check the bag
> when you check in for the flight. Retrieve the bag in Miami
> before you make your connection. Give it to the uniformed
> courier representative, who'll await you beyond customs.

No company makes such offers anymore. But this was 1985—
years before intense airport security. My dad was dying of ALS,
airline tickets were expensive, and my checking account was as
thin as a Paris supermodel. Free ticket? The offer sounded too
good to be true.

So I walked away from it.

Many do the same with John 3:16. Millions read the verse. Only a handful trust it. Wary of a catch perhaps? Not needy enough maybe? Cautioned by guarded friends?

I was. Other Rio residents saw the same offer. Some read it and smelled a rat. "Don't risk it," one warned me. "Better to buy your own ticket."

But I couldn't afford one. Each call to Mom brought worse news.

"He's back in the hospital."

"Unable to breathe without oxygen."

"The doctor says it's time to call hospice."

So I revisited the flyer. Desperation heightened my interest.

Doesn't it always?

When he asks for a divorce or she says, "It's over." When the coroner calls, the kids rebel, or the finances collapse. When desperation typhoons into your world, God's offer of a free flight home demands a second look. John 3:16 morphs from a nice verse to a life vest.

Some of you are wearing it. You can recount the day you put it on. For you, the passage comforts like your favorite blanket:

> God so loved . . .
> believes in him . . .
> shall not perish . . .
> eternal life.

These words have kept you company through multiple wind-swept winters. I pray they warm you through the ones that remain.

Others of you are still studying the flyer. Still pondering the possibility, wrestling with the promise. One day wondering what kind of fool offer this is, the next wondering what kind of fool would turn it down.

I urge you not to. Don't walk away from this one. Who else can get you home? Who else has turned his grave into a changing closet and offered to do the same with yours? Take Jesus's offer. Get on board. You don't want to miss this chance to see your Father.

I didn't. I called the company and signed up. Denalyn drove me to the airport. I found the courier employee, accepted the passage, checked the bag, and took my seat on the plane, smiling as though I'd just found a forgotten gift under the Christmas tree.

Do likewise. You don't need to go to the airport, but you do need to make a move. You need to give God your answer: "Christ will live in you as you open the door and invite him in" (Eph. 3:17 MSG). Say yes to him. Your prayer needs no eloquence, just honesty.

Father, I believe you love this world. You gave your one and only Son so I can live forever with you. Apart from you, I die. With you, I live. I choose life. I choose you.

If you aren't sure you've told him, you haven't. We can't get on board and not know it. Nor can we get on board and hide it. No stowaways permitted. Christ-followers go public with their belief. We turn from bad behavior to good (repentance). We stop following our passions and salute our new captain (confession). We publicly demonstrate our devotion (baptism).[1]

We don't keep our choice a secret. Why would we? We're on our way home for Christ's sake.

Thanks to the courier folks, I was present at my father's death.

Thanks to God, he'll be present at yours. He cares too much not to be. Believe in him and you

> will . . .

> > not . . .

> > > perish.

You will have life, eternal life, forever.

Only Jesus:

40 Days
with the Son

AN INVITATION
FROM MAX

The story of Jesus reads a bit like a scrapbook. Headline clippings. Newspaper photos. Jesus's favorite stories and lesson outlines. Here's Luke's snapshot of Jesus riding in Peter's boat. Matthew took this group photo when the seventy followers met for a party after the first mission trip. (Jesus is the one seated cross-legged in the center of the first row, smiling like his troop captured the Boy Scout Jamboree trophy.) John pasted a wedding napkin from Cana in the book as well as a funeral program from Bethany. He was the contributor who lamented, "There are so many other things Jesus did. If they were all written down, each of them, one by one, I can't imagine a world big enough to hold such a library of books" (John 21:25 MSG).

Flipping through the scrapbook leaves the reader with this impression: Jesus was, at once, common and not; alternately normal and heroic. One minute blending in with the domino players in the park, the next commanding the hell out of madmen, disease out of the dying, and death out of the dead. He conversed with kids and fishermen yet spoke with equal ease to waves, wind gusts, and demons. Who was this man?

No question matters more. I've collected a few scrapbook

entries to help us find an answer. Having dedicated the book to the deep drilling of one of Jesus's statements, I want us to conclude with a flyby read of his entire life. Consider reading one entry a day for the next forty days, from the Bethlehem manger to the vacated tomb. Keep in mind that the final entries are yet to come, including the snapshot of you and your Savior at heaven's gateway.

DAY 1

AN EXTRA-ORDINARY NIGHT

"Suddenly a great company of the heavenly host
appeared with the angel, praising God and saying,
'Glory to God in the highest, and on earth
peace to men on whom his favor rests.'"
—LUKE 2:13–14

There is one word that describes the night he came—*ordinary*.

The sky was ordinary. An occasional gust stirred the leaves and chilled the air. The stars were diamonds sparkling on black velvet.

The sheep were ordinary. Some fat. Some scrawny. Common animals. No history makers. No blue-ribbon winners.

And the shepherds. Peasants they were. Probably wearing all the clothes they owned. Smelling like sheep and looking just as woolly.

An ordinary night with ordinary sheep and ordinary shepherds. And were it not for a God who loves to hook an "extra" on the front of the ordinary, the night would have gone un-noticed. The sheep would have been forgotten, and the shep-herds would have slept the night away.

But God dances amidst the common. And that night he did a waltz.

The black sky exploded with brightness. Trees that had been shadows jumped into clarity. Sheep that had been silent became a chorus of curiosity. One minute the shepherd was dead asleep; the next he was rubbing his eyes and staring into the face of an alien.

The night was ordinary no more.

The announcement went first to the shepherds. Had the angel gone to the theologians, they would have first consulted their commentaries. Had he gone to the elite, they would have looked around to see if anyone was watching.

So he went to the shepherds. Men who didn't know enough to tell God that angels don't sing to sheep and that messiahs aren't found wrapped in rags and sleeping in a feed trough.

DAY 2

MARY CRADLES GOD

"And she gave birth to her firstborn, a son.
She wrapped him in cloths and
placed him in a manger, because
there was no room for them in the inn."
—LUKE 2:7

God had entered the world as a baby.

Yet, were someone to chance upon the sheep stable on the outskirts of Bethlehem that morning, what a peculiar scene they would behold.

The stable stinks like all stables do. The ground is hard, the hay scarce. Cobwebs cling to the ceiling, and a mouse scurries across the dirt floor.

A more lowly place of birth could not exist.

Near the young mother sits the weary father. If anyone is dozing, he is. He can't remember the last time he sat down. And now that the excitement has subsided a bit, now that Mary and the baby are comfortable, he leans against the wall of the stable and feels his eyes grow heavy.

Wide awake is Mary. My, how young she looks! Her head rests on the soft leather of Joseph's saddle. The pain has been eclipsed by wonder. She looks into the face of the baby. Her son. Her Lord. His Majesty. At this point in history, the human being who best understands who God is and what he is doing is a teenage girl in a smelly stable. She can't take her eyes off him. Mary knows she is holding God. She remembers the words of the angel: "His kingdom will never end" (Luke 1:33).

He looks like anything but a king. His face is prunish and red. He is absolutely dependent upon Mary for his well-being.

Majesty in the midst of the mundane. She touches the face of the infant-God. *How long was your journey!*

DAY 3

JOSEPH, CAUGHT IN THE MIDDLE

"When Joseph woke up, he did what the
angel of the Lord had commanded him
and took Mary home as his wife. But he had no
union with her until she gave birth to a son.
And he gave him the name Jesus."
—MATTHEW 1:24–25

Matthew describes Jesus's earthly father as a craftsman (Matt. 13:55). A small-town carpenter, he lives in Nazareth: a single-camel map dot on the edge of boredom. Is he the right choice? Doesn't God have better options? An eloquent priest from Jerusalem or a scholar from the Pharisees? Why Joseph? A major part of the answer lies in his reputation: he gives it up for Jesus. "Then Joseph [Mary's] husband, being a just man, and not wanting to make her a public example, was minded to put her away secretly" (Matt. 1:19 NKJV).

With the phrase "a just man," Matthew recognizes the status of Joseph. Nazareth viewed him as we might view an elder, deacon, or Bible class teacher. Joseph likely took pride in his standing, but Mary's announcement jeopardized it. *I'm pregnant.*

Now what? His fiancée is blemished, tainted . . . he is righteous, godly. On one hand, he has the law. On the other, he has his love. The law says, stone her. Love says, forgive her. Joseph is caught in the middle.

Then comes the angel. Mary's growing belly gives no cause for concern, but reason to rejoice. "She carries the Son of God in her womb," the angel announces. But who would believe it?

A bead of sweat forms beneath Joseph's beard. He faces a dilemma. Make up a lie and preserve his place in the community, or tell the truth and kiss his reputation good-bye. He makes his decision. "Joseph . . . took to him his wife, and did not know her till she had brought forth her firstborn Son" (Matt. 1:24–25 NKJV).

Joseph swapped his Torah studies for a pregnant fiancée and an illegitimate son and made the big decision of discipleship. He placed God's plan ahead of his own.

DAY 4

BECAUSE OF LOVE

"For God so loved the world that he gave
his one and only Son, that whoever believes
in him shall not perish but have eternal life."
—JOHN 3:16

Would you do what Jesus did? He swapped a spotless castle for a grimy stable. He exchanged the worship of angels for the company of killers. He could hold the universe in his palm but gave it up to float in the womb of a maiden.

If you were God, would you sleep on straw, nurse from a breast, and be clothed in a diaper? I wouldn't, but Christ did.

If you knew that those you loved would laugh in your face, would you still care? . . . Christ did.

He humbled himself. He went from commanding angels to sleeping in the straw. From holding stars to clutching Mary's finger. The palm that held the universe took the nail of a soldier.

Why? Because that's what love does. It puts the beloved before itself.

Love goes the distance . . . and Christ traveled from limitless eternity to be confined by time in order to become one of us. He didn't have to. He could have given up. At any step along the way, he could have called it quits.

When he saw the size of the womb, he could have stopped.

When he saw how tiny his hand would be, how soft his voice would be, how hungry his tummy would be, he could have stopped. At the first whiff of the stinky stable, at the first gust of cold air. The first time he scraped his knee or blew his nose or tasted burnt bagels, he could have turned and walked out.

When he saw the dirt floor of his Nazareth house. When Joseph gave him a chore to do. When his fellow students were dozing off during the reading of the Torah, his Torah. At any point Jesus could have said, "That's it! That's enough! I'm going home." But he didn't.

He didn't, because he is love.

DAY 5

JESUS GOES HOME FIRST

"And the child grew and became strong;
he was filled with wisdom,
and the grace of God was upon him."
—LUKE 2:40

When do we get our first clue that Jesus knows he is the Son of God? In the temple of Jerusalem. He is twelve years old. His parents are three days into the return trip to Nazareth before they notice he is missing.

The temple is the last place they think to search. But it is the first place Jesus goes. He doesn't go to a cousin's house or a buddy's playground. Jesus seeks the place of godly thinking and, in doing so, inspires us to do the same. By the time Joseph and Mary locate their son, he has confounded the most learned men in the temple.

As a young boy, Jesus already senses the call of God. But what does he do next? Recruit apostles and preach sermons and perform miracles? No, he goes home to his folks and learns the family business.

That is exactly what you should do. Want to bring focus to your life? Do what Jesus did. Go home, love your family, and take care of business. *But, Max, I want to be a missionary.* Your first mission field is under your roof. What makes you think they'll believe you overseas if they don't believe you across the hall?

DAY 6

CHICKENS, HAMMER, AND JESUS

"He's just a carpenter."
—MARK 6:3 (MSG)

Envision a dusty, quiet village. Nazareth. An unimpressive town in an unimpressive nation.

Ignore the nicer homes of the village. Joseph and Mary celebrated the birth of Jesus with a temple offering of two turtledoves, the gift of the poor (Luke 2:22–24). Go to the poorer part of town. Not poverty stricken or destitute, just simple.

And look for a single mom. The absence of Joseph in the adult life of Jesus suggests that Mary may have raised him and the rest of the kids alone. We need a simple home with a single mom and an ordinary laborer. Jesus's neighbors remembered him as a worker. "He's just a carpenter" (Mark 6:3 MSG).

Jesus had dirty hands, sweat-stained shirts, and—this may

surprise you—common looks. "No stately form or majesty that we should look upon Him, nor appearance that we should be attracted to Him" (Isa. 53:2 NASB).

Raised in an overlooked nation among oppressed people in an obscure village. Can you spot him? See the adobe house with the thatched roof? Yes, the one with the chickens in the yard and the gangly teenager repairing chairs in the shed.

"He had to enter into every detail of human life. Then, when he came before God as high priest to get rid of the people's sins, he would have already experienced it all himself—all the pain, all the testing—and would be able to help where help was needed" (Heb. 2:17–18 MSG).

Why would heaven's finest Son endure earth's toughest pain? So you would know that he knows how you feel.

DAY 7

GOOD-BYE, NAZARETH

*"Jesus went into Galilee,
proclaiming the good news of God."*
—MARK 1:14

Jesus's obedience began in a small town carpentry shop. His uncommon approach to his common life groomed him for his uncommon call. "When Jesus entered public life he was about thirty years old" (Luke 3:23 MSG). In order to enter public life, you have to leave private life. In order for Jesus to change the world, he had to say good-bye to *his* world.

He had to give Mary a kiss. Have a final meal in the kitchen, a final walk through the streets. Did he ascend one of the hills of Nazareth and think of the day he would ascend the hill near Jerusalem?

He knew what was going to happen. "God chose him for this purpose long before the world began" (1 Pet. 1:20 NLT). Every ounce of suffering had been scripted—it just fell to him to play the part.

Not that he had to. Nazareth was a cozy town. Why not build a carpentry business? Keep his identity a secret? Return in the era of guillotines or electric chairs, and pass on the cross. To be forced to die is one thing, but to willingly take up your own cross is something else.

I wonder, what kind of love is this? When you come up with a word for such a love, give it to Christ. For the day he left Nazareth is the day he declared his devotion for you and me. According to Peter, our lives were a "dead-end, empty-headed" (1 Pet. 1:18 MSG). But God, "immense in mercy and with an incredible love . . . embraced us" (Eph. 2:4 MSG).

Jesus left Nazareth and brought us to life.

DAY 8

🍂 🍂

BAPTIZE YOU?

"As soon as Jesus was baptized, he went up
out of the water. At that moment heaven was
opened, and he saw the Spirit of God
descending like a dove and lighting on him.
And a voice from heaven said, 'This is my Son,
whom I love; with him I am well pleased.'"
—MATTHEW 3:16–17

Nothing in his appearance separates him from the crowd. Like the rest, he is standing in line, waiting his turn. He, like the others, can hear the voice of the preacher in the distance.

Between baptisms, John the Baptist is prone to preach. Impetuous. Fiery. Bronzed face, unshorn locks. He stands waist-deep in the cobalt-colored Jordan. He makes a point of calling all people to the water. "He went into all the country around the

Jordan, preaching a baptism of repentance for the forgiveness of sins" (Luke 3:3).

Baptism wasn't a new practice. It was a required rite for any Gentile seeking to become a Jew. Baptism was for the moldy, second-class, unchosen people, not the clean, top-of-the-line class favorites—the Jews. Herein lies the rub. John refuses to delineate between Jew and Gentile. In his book, every heart needs a detail job.

Every heart, that is, except one. That's why John is stunned when that one wades into the river.

John's reluctance is understandable. A baptismal ceremony is an odd place to find the Son of God. He should be the baptizer not the baptizee. Why would Christ want to be baptized? Why would he need to be baptized?

Here's why: Since you and I cannot pay, Christ did. We've broken commandments, promises, and, worst of all, we've broken God's heart.

But Christ sees our plight. We owe God a perfect life. Perfect obedience to every command. Not just the command of baptism, but the commands of humility, honesty, integrity. We can't deliver. Might as well charge us for the property of Manhattan. But Christ can and he did. His plunge into the Jordan is a picture of his plunge into our sin. His baptism announces, "Let me pay."

Your baptism responds, "You bet I will."

DAY 9

SATAN STALKED HIM

"He faced all of the same temptations we do."
—HEBREWS 4:15 (NLT)

You and I know what it is like to endure a moment of temptation or an hour of temptation, even a day of temptation. But *forty* days? That is what Jesus faced. "The Spirit led Jesus into the desert where the devil tempted Jesus for forty days" (Luke 4:1–2 NCV).

We imagine the wilderness temptation as three isolated events scattered over a forty-day period. Would that it had been. In reality, Jesus's time of testing was nonstop; "the devil tempted Jesus for forty days." Satan got on Jesus like a shirt and refused to leave. Every step, whispering in his ear. Every turn of the path, sowing doubt. Was Jesus impacted by the devil? Apparently so. Luke doesn't say that Satan *tried* to tempt Jesus. No, the passage is clear: "the devil tempted Jesus." Jesus was *tempted*; he was tested. Tempted to change sides? Tempted to go home? Tempted to settle for a kingdom on earth? I don't know, but I know he was tempted. A war raged within. Stress stormed without.

Like Jesus we are tempted. Like Jesus we are accused. But unlike Jesus, we give up. We give out. We sit down. How can our hearts have the endurance Jesus had?

By focusing where Jesus focused: on "the joy that God put before him" (Heb. 12:2 NCV). He lifted his eyes beyond the horizon and saw the table. He focused on the feast. And what he saw gave him strength to finish—and finish strong.

Such a moment awaits us. In an hour that has no end, we will rest. Surrounded by saints and engulfed by Jesus himself, the work will, indeed, be finished. The final harvest will have been gathered, we will be seated, and Christ will christen the meal with these words: "Well done, good and faithful servant" (Matt. 25:23 KJV).

DAY 10

BIFOCALS AND BINOCULARS

"We have found the Messiah."
—JOHN 1:41

For John and Andrew, it wasn't enough to listen to John the Baptist. Most would have been content to serve in the shadow of the world's most famous evangelist. Could there be a better teacher? Only one. And when John and Andrew saw him, they left John the Baptist and followed Jesus. Note the request they made.

"Rabbi," they asked, "where are you staying?" (John 1:38 NCV). Pretty bold request. They didn't ask Jesus to give them a minute or an opinion or a message or a miracle. They asked for his address. They wanted to hang out with him. They wanted to know him. They wanted to know what caused his head to turn and his heart to burn and his soul to yearn. They wanted to study his eyes and follow his steps. They wanted to see him. They wanted to know what made him laugh and if he ever got tired.

And most of all, they wanted to know, *Could Jesus be who John said he was—and if he is, what on earth is God doing on the earth?* You can't answer such a question by talking to his cousin; you've got to talk to the man himself.

Jesus's answer to the disciples? "Come and see" (v. 39 NCV). He didn't say, "Come and glance" or "Come and peek." He said, "Come and see." Bring your bifocals and binoculars. There is no time for side-glances or occasional peeks. "Let us fix our eyes on Jesus, the author and perfecter of our faith" (Heb. 12:2).

The disciple fixes his eyes on the Savior.

DAY 11

ALMIGHTY—NOT HIGH AND MIGHTY

"Both Jesus and His disciples
were invited to the wedding."
—JOHN 2:2 (NKJV)

Maybe it was Andrew who asked it. Perhaps Peter. Could be that all approached Jesus. But I wager that at some point in Jesus's first journey, the disciples expressed their assumptions.

"So, Rabbi, where are you taking us? To the desert?"

"No," opines another, "he's taking us to the temple."

Then a chorus of confusion breaks out and ends only when Jesus lifts his hand and says softly, "We're on our way to a wedding."

Silence. John and Andrew look at each other. "A wedding?" they say.

Why did Jesus go to the wedding?

The answer? It's found in the second verse of John 2. "Jesus and his followers were also invited to the wedding" (NCV).

When the bride and groom were putting the guest list together, Jesus's name was included. Jesus wasn't invited because he was a celebrity. He wasn't one yet. The invitation wasn't motivated by his miracles. He'd yet to perform any. Why did they invite him?

I suppose they liked him.

Big deal? I think so. I think it's significant that common folk in a little town enjoyed being with Jesus. I think it's noteworthy that the Almighty didn't act high and mighty.

He went to great pains to be as human as the guy down the street. He didn't need to study, but still went to the synagogue. He had no need for income, but still worked in the workshop. Upon his shoulders rested the challenge of redeeming creation, but he still took time to walk ninety miles from Jericho to Cana to go to a wedding.

As a result, people liked him.

DAY 12

JUST CALL HER GRACE

"He knows me inside and out!"
—JOHN 4:39 (MSG)

Talk about a woman who could make a list. Number one, discrimination. She is a Samaritan, hated by Jews. Number two, gender bias. She is a female, condescended to by the men. Third, she is a divorcée, not once, not twice. Let's see if we can count. Four? Five? Five marriages turned south, and now she's sharing a bed with a guy who won't give her a ring.

When I add this up, I envision a happy-hour stool sitter who lives with her mad at half boil. Husky voice, cigarette breath, and a dress cut low at the top and high at the bottom. Certainly not Samaria's finest. Certainly not the woman you'd put in charge of the Ladies' Bible class.

Which makes the fact that Jesus does just that all the more surprising. He doesn't just put her in charge of the class; he puts her in charge of evangelizing the whole town. Before the day is over, the entire city hears about a man who claims to be God. "He told me everything I ever did" (John 4:39), she tells them, leaving unsaid the obvious, "and he loved me anyway."

A little rain can straighten a flower stem. A little love can change a life. Who knew the last time this woman had been entrusted with anything, much less the biggest news in history!

Listen. You have not been sprinkled with forgiveness. You have not been spattered with grace. You are submerged in mercy. Let it change you! See if God's love doesn't do for you what it did for the woman in Samaria. He found her full of trash and left her full of grace.

DAY 13

CHRIST'S CRAZY KIN

"And he was amazed at their lack of faith."
—MARK 6:6

It may surprise you to know that Jesus's family was less than perfect. They were. If your family doesn't appreciate you, take heart; neither did Jesus's. "A prophet is honored everywhere except in his hometown and with his own people and in his own home" (Mark 6:4 NCV).

One minute he was a hero, the next a heretic. When his neighborhood friends tried to kill him . . . his brothers were invisible. They thought their brother was a lunatic. "His family . . . went to get him because they thought he was out of his mind" (Mark 3:21 NCV). They weren't proud—they were embarrassed!

How did Jesus put up with these guys? When you and your family have two different agendas, what do you do?

Jesus gives us some answers.

It's worth noting that he didn't try to control his family's behavior, nor did he let their behavior control his. He didn't demand that they agree with him. He didn't sulk when they insulted him. He didn't make it his mission to try to please them.

When Jesus's brothers didn't share his convictions, he didn't try to force them. He recognized that his spiritual family could provide what his physical family didn't. He didn't let the difficult dynamic of his family overshadow his call from God.

Day 14

Too Early to Retire

*"Do not conform any longer to the pattern
of this world, but be transformed by the
renewing of your mind. Then you will be
able to test and approve what God's will is—
his good, pleasing and perfect will."*

—Romans 12:2

Having withstood the devil's wilderness temptations and his hometown's harsh rejection, Jesus journeyed to Capernaum, where the citizens gave him a ticker-tape reception. "They were astonished at His teaching" (Luke 4:32 NKJV).

But the people brought Jesus more than sick bodies and seeking souls. They brought him agendas. Itineraries. Unsolicited advice. The herd of humanity wanted to set Jesus's course. "Heed us," they said. "We'll direct your steps."

The people of Capernaum "tried to keep Him from leaving

them; but He said to them, 'I must preach the kingdom of God to the other cities also, because for this purpose I have been sent'" (vv. 42–43 NKJV).

He resisted the undertow of the people by anchoring to the rock of his purpose: employing his uniqueness (to "preach . . . to the other cities also") to make a big deal out of God ("the kingdom of God") everywhere he could.

And aren't you glad he did? Suppose he had heeded the crowd and set up camp in Capernaum, reasoning, "I thought the whole world was my target and the cross my destiny. But the entire town tells me to stay in Capernaum. Could all these people be wrong?"

Yes, they could! In defiance of the crowd, Jesus turned his back on the Capernaum pastorate and followed the will of God. Doing so meant leaving some sick people unhealed and some confused people untaught. He said no to good things so he could say yes to the right thing: his unique call.

Day 15

When Jesus Gets into Your Boat

"They caught such a large number of fish
that their nets began to break."
—Luke 5:6

Jesus needs a boat; Peter provides one. Jesus preaches; Peter is content to listen. Jesus suggests a midmorning fishing trip, however, and Peter gives him a look. The it's-too-late look. He runs his fingers through his hair and sighs, "Master, we worked hard all night and caught nothing" (Luke 5:5 NASB). Can you feel Peter's futility?

Oh the thoughts Peter might have had. *I'm tired. Bone tired. I want a meal and a bed, not a fishing trip.*

"Put out into the deep water," the God-man instructs. Why the deep water? You suppose Jesus knew something Peter didn't?

Finding fish is simple for the God who made them. To Jesus, the Sea of Galilee is a dollar-store fishbowl on a kitchen cabinet.

I like to think that Peter, while holding the net, looks over his shoulder at Jesus. And I like to think that Jesus, knowing Peter is about to be half yanked into the water, starts to smile.

Peter's arm is pulled into the water. It's all he can do to hang on until the other guys can help. Within moments the four fishermen and the carpenter are up to their knees in flopping silver.

Peter lifts his eyes off the catch and onto the face of Christ. In that moment, for the first time, he sees Jesus. Not Jesus the Fish Finder. Not Jesus the Rabbi. Peter sees Jesus the Lord.

Peter falls face-first among the fish. Their stink doesn't bother him. It is his stink that he's worried about. "Depart from me, for I am a sinful man, O Lord!" (v. 8 NASB).

Christ had no intention of honoring that request. He doesn't abandon self-confessed schlemiels. Quite the contrary, he enlists them. "Do not fear, from now on you will be catching men" (v. 10 NASB).

DAY 16

CHUMMING WITH THE MAFIA

"I'm here to invite outsiders, not coddle insiders."
—MATTHEW 9:13 (MSG)

According to his résumé, Matthew was a revenue consultant for the government. According to his neighbors, he was a crook. He kept a tax booth and a hand extended at the street corner. That's where he was the day he saw Jesus. "Follow me," the Master said, and Matthew did. And in the very next verse we find Jesus sitting at Matthew's dining room table. "Jesus was having dinner at Matthew's house" (Matt. 9:10 NCV).

A curbside conversion couldn't satisfy his heart, so Matthew took Jesus home. Something happens over a dinner table that doesn't happen over an office desk. Take off the tie, heat up the grill, break out the sodas, and spend the evening with the suspender of the stars. "You know, Jesus, forgive me for asking, but I've always wanted to know . . ."

Though the giving of the invitation is impressive, the acceptance is more so. Didn't matter to Jesus that Matthew was a thief. Didn't matter to Jesus that Matthew had built a split-level house with the proceeds of extortion. What did matter was that Matthew wanted to know Jesus.

The ratio between those who missed Jesus and those who sought him is thousands to one. But the ratio between those who sought him and those who found him was one to one. All who sought him found him.

DAY 17

STANDING ON HIS WORD

"Now there is in Jerusalem near the
Sheep Gate a pool. . . . Here a great number
of disabled people used to lie."
—JOHN 5:2–3

Jesus encounters a paralyzed man near a large pool north of the temple in Jerusalem. It's 360 feet long, 130 feet wide, and 75 feet deep. A colonnade with five porches overlooks the body of water.

It's called Bethesda. An underwater spring causes the pool to bubble occasionally. The people believe the bubbles are caused by the dipping of angels' wings. They also believe that the first person to touch the water after the angel does will be healed.

Picture a battleground strewn with wounded bodies, and you see Bethesda. An endless wave of groans. A field of faceless need. Most people walk past, ignoring the hurting.

But not Jesus. He is in Jerusalem for a feast. He is alone. He's not there to teach the disciples or to draw a crowd. The people need him—so he's there.

Can you picture it? Jesus walking among the suffering? People have come from miles around to meet God in the temple. Little do they know that he is with the sick. Little do they know that the strong young carpenter who surveys the ragged landscape of pain is God.

Before Jesus heals the paralytic, he asks him a question: "Do you want to be well?"

"Sir, there is no one to help me get into the pool when the water starts moving" (John 5:6–7 NCV).

Is the fellow complaining? Who knows. But before we think about it too much, look what happens next.

"'Stand up. Pick up your mat and walk.' And immediately the man was well; he picked up his mat and began to walk" (vv. 8–9 NCV).

I wish we would do that. I wish we would learn that when Jesus says something, it happens. When Jesus tells us to stand, let's stand.

DAY 18

THE GOD-MAN JESUS

"What kind of man is this?"
—MATTHEW 8:27

Most people stand quietly as funeral processions pass. Mouths closed. Hands folded. Reverently silent. Not Jesus. Not that day in Nain. He approached the mother of the dead boy and whispered something in her ear that made her turn and look at her son. She started to object but didn't. Signaling to the pallbearers, Jesus instructed, "Wait."

He walked toward the boy. Eye level with the corpse, he spoke. Not over it, as a prayer, but to it, as a command. "Young man, I say to you, arise!" (Luke 7:14 NASB).

With the tone of a teacher telling students to sit or the authority of a mom telling kids to get out of the rain, Jesus commanded the dead boy *not to be dead.* And the boy obeyed. Cold skin warmed. Stiff limbs moved. White cheeks flushed. The men lowered the coffin, and the boy jumped up and into his mother's arms. Jesus "gave him back to his mother" (Luke 7:15).

An hour later Jesus and the guys were eating the evening meal. He laughed at a joke and asked for seconds on bread, and the irony of it all jolted Peter. *Who are you?* he wondered so softly that no one but God could hear. *You just awakened the dead! Should you not be encased in light or encircled by angels or enthroned higher than a thousand Caesars? Yet, look at you— laughing at jokes I tell and eating the food we all eat. Just who are you?*

He was, at once, man and God. Don't we need a God-man Savior? A just-God Jesus could make us but not understand us. A just-man Jesus could love us but never save us. But a God-man Jesus? Near enough to touch. Strong enough to trust. A next-door Savior.

DAY 19

THE WAVES ARE LISTENING

"Even the wind and the waves obey him!"
—MARK 4:41

Jesus and the disciples are in a boat crossing the Sea of Galilee. A storm arises suddenly, and what was placid becomes violent—monstrous waves rise out of the sea and slap the boat. Mark describes it clearly: "A furious squall came up, and the waves broke over the boat, so that it was nearly swamped" (Mark 4:37).

Imagine yourself in the boat. It's a sturdy vessel, but no match for these ten-foot waves. It plunges nose first into the wall of water. The force of the wave dangerously tips the boat until the bow seems to be pointing straight at the sky. A dozen sets of hands join yours in clutching the mast. All your shipmates have wet heads and wide eyes. You tune your ear for a calming voice, but all you hear are screams and prayers. All of a sudden it hits you—someone is missing. Where is Jesus? He's not at the mast.

He's not grabbing the edge. Where is he? You turn and look, and there curled in the stern of the boat is Jesus, sleeping!

You don't know whether to be amazed or angry, so you're both. How can he sleep at a time like this? How could he sleep through the storm?

Simple, he was in charge of it.

Jesus "got up, rebuked the wind and said to the waves, 'Quiet! Be still!' Then the wind died down and it was completely calm" (v. 39). The raging water becomes a stilled sea, instantly. Immediate calm. Not a ripple.

The waves were his subjects, and the winds were his servants. The whole universe was his kingdom.

DAY 20

THE HAND HE LOVES TO HOLD

"Daughter, your faith has healed you. Go in peace
and be freed from your suffering."
—MARK 5:34

Can you see it? Her hand? Gnarled. Thin. Diseased. Dirt black-
ens the nails and stains the skin. Look carefully amid the knees
and feet of the crowd. They're scampering after Christ. He
walks. She crawls. People bump her, but she doesn't stop. Others
complain. She doesn't care. The woman is desperate. Blood
won't stay in her body. "There was a woman in the crowd who
had had a hemorrhage for twelve years" (Mark 5:25 NLT).

She has nothing. No money. No home. No health. Dilapi-
dated dreams. Deflated faith. Unwelcome in the synagogue. Unwanted by her community. For twelve years she has suffered. She
is desperate. And her desperation births an idea.

"She had heard about Jesus" (v. 27 NLT). Every society has a grapevine, even—or especially—the society of the sick. Word among the lepers and the left out is this: Jesus can heal. And Jesus is coming. By invitation of the synagogue ruler, Jesus is coming to Capernaum.

As the crowd comes, she thinks, "If I can just touch his clothing, I will be healed" (v. 28 NLT). At the right time, she crab-scurries through the crowd. Knees bump her ribs. "Move out of the way!" someone shouts. She doesn't care and doesn't stop.

She touches the robe of Jesus, and "immediately the bleeding stopped, and she could feel that she had been healed!" (v. 29 NLT). Life rushes in. Pale cheeks turn pink. Shallow breaths become full.

Illness took her strength. What took yours? Red ink? Hard drink? Late nights in the wrong arms? Long days on the wrong job? Pregnant too soon? Too often? Is her hand your hand? If so, take heart. Christ wants to touch it. When your hand reaches through the masses, he knows.

Yours is the hand he loves to hold.

DAY 21

WHEN GOD SIGHS

*"He looked up to heaven and with a
deep sigh said to him, 'Ephphatha!'
(which means, 'Be opened!')."*
—MARK 7:34

Perhaps he stammered. Maybe he spoke with a lisp. Perhaps, because of his deafness, he never learned to articulate words properly.

Jesus, refusing to exploit the situation, took the man aside. He looked him in the face. Knowing it would be useless to talk, he explained what he was about to do through gestures. He spat and touched the man's tongue, telling him that whatever restricted his speech was about to be removed. He touched his ears. They, for the first time, were about to hear.

But before the man said a word or heard a sound, Jesus did something I never would have anticipated.

175

He sighed.

I'd never thought of God as one who sighs. I'd thought of God as one who commands. I'd thought of God as one who called forth the dead with a command or created the universe with a word . . . but a God who sighs?

When Jesus looked into the eyes of Satan's victim, the only appropriate thing to do was sigh. "It was never intended to be this way," the sigh said. "Your ears weren't made to be deaf; your tongue wasn't made to stumble." The imbalance of it all caused the Master to languish.

And in the agony of Jesus lies our hope. Had he not sighed, we would be in a pitiful condition. Had he simply chalked it all up to the inevitable or washed his hands of the whole stinking mess, what hope would we have?

But he didn't. That holy sigh assures us that God still groans for his people. He groans for the day when all sighs will cease, when what was intended to be will be.

DAY 22

NOT GUILTY

"Whoever follows me will never walk in darkness,
but will have the light of life."
—JOHN 8:12

The woman stands in the center of the circle. Those men around her are religious leaders. Pharisees, they are called. Self-appointed custodians of conduct. And the other man—the one in the simple clothes, the one sitting on the ground, the one looking at the face of the woman—that's Jesus.

Jesus has been teaching. The woman has been cheating. And the Pharisees are out to stop them both.

"Teacher, this woman was caught in the act of adultery" (John 8:4). In an instant she is yanked from private passion to public spectacle. Nothing can hide her shame. From this second on, she'll be known as an adulteress. When she goes to the market, women will whisper. When she passes, heads will turn.

"The law of Moses commands that we stone to death every woman who does this. What do you say we should do?" (v. 5 NCV).

What does Jesus do? Jesus writes in the sand. And after he writes, he speaks: "Anyone here who has never sinned can throw the first stone at her" (v. 7 NCV).

The young look to the old. The old look in their hearts. They are the first to drop their stones.

"Woman, where are they? Has no one judged you guilty?"

She answers, "No one, sir."

Then Jesus says, "I also don't judge you guilty. You may go now, but don't sin anymore" (vv. 10–11 NCV).

If you have ever wondered how God reacts when you fail, watch carefully. He's writing. He's leaving a message. Not in the sand, but on a cross. His message has two words: not guilty.

DAY 23

✦ ✦

JESUS VS. DEATH

"Then Jesus said, 'Did I not tell you that if you believed, you would see the glory of God?'"
—JOHN 11:40

In this scene there are two people: Martha and Jesus.

Her words are full of despair. "If you had been here . . ." (John 11:21). She stares into the Master's face with confused eyes. Her brother Lazarus is dead. And the one man who could have made a difference didn't. Something about death makes us accuse God of betrayal. "If God were here, there would be no death!" we claim.

You see, if God is God anywhere, he has to be God in the face of death. Pop psychology can deal with depression. Prosperity can handle hunger. But only God can deal with our ultimate dilemma— death. And only the God of the Bible has dared to stand on the canyon's edge and offer an answer. He has to be God in the face of death. If not, he is not God anywhere.

Perhaps it is Jesus's patience that causes Martha to change her tone from frustration to earnestness. "Even now God will give you whatever you ask" (v. 22).

Jesus then makes one of those claims that place him either on the throne or in the asylum: "Your brother will rise again" (v. 23).

Jesus's words echo off the canyon walls. "I am the resurrection and the life. He who believes in me will live, even though he dies; and whoever lives and believes in me will never die" (vv. 25–26).

It is a hinge point in history. With eyes locked on hers, he asks the greatest question found in Scripture.

"Do you believe this?" (v. 26).

There it is. The question that drives any responsible listener to absolute obedience to or total rejection of the Christian faith.

DAY 24

JESUS MINDS HIS MIND

"Jesus often withdrew to
lonely places and prayed."
—LUKE 5:16

Jesus stubbornly guarded the gateway of his heart. Many thoughts were denied entrance. Need a few examples?

How about arrogance? On one occasion the people determined to make Jesus their king. What an attractive thought. Most of us would delight in the notion of royalty. Not Jesus. "Jesus saw that in their enthusiasm, they were about to grab him and make him king, so he slipped off and went back up the mountain to be by himself" (John 6:15 MSG).

Another dramatic example occurred in a conversation Jesus had with Peter. Upon hearing Jesus announce his impending death on the cross, the impetuous apostle objected. "Impossible, Master! That can never be!" (Matt. 16:22 MSG). Apparently,

Peter was about to question the necessity of Calvary. But he never had a chance. Christ blocked the doorway. He sent both the messenger and the author of the heresy scurrying: "Peter, get out of my way. Satan, get lost. You have no idea how God works" (v. 23 MSG).

And how about the time Jesus was mocked? Responding to an appeal to heal a sick girl, he entered her house only to be told she was dead. His response? "The child is not dead but sleeping." The response of the people in the house? "They laughed at him." Just like all of us, Jesus had to face a moment of humiliation. But unlike most of us, he refused to receive it. Note his decisive response: "he put them all outside" (Mark 5:39–40 RSV). The mockery was not allowed in the house of the girl nor in the mind of Christ.

Jesus guarded his heart. If he did, shouldn't we do the same?

DAY 25

STEP IN THE BASIN

*"Whoever acknowledges me before men, I will also
acknowledge him before my Father in heaven."*
—MATTHEW 10:32

It's not easy watching Jesus wash these feet.

To see the hands of God massaging the toes of men is,
well . . . it's not right. The disciples should be washing his feet.
Nathanael should pour the water. Andrew should carry the
towel. But they don't. No one does. Rather than serve, they
argue over which one is the greatest (Luke 22:24).

As they bicker, Jesus stands. He removes his robe and takes
the servant's wrap off of the wall. Taking the pitcher, he pours
the water into the basin. He kneels before them with the basin
and sponge and begins to wash. The towel that covers his waist
is also the towel that dries their feet.

It's not right.

Isn't it enough that these hands will be pierced in the morning? Must they scrub grime tonight? And the disciples . . . do they deserve to have their feet washed?

Look around the table, Jesus. Out of the twelve, how many will stand with you in Pilate's court? How many will share with you the Roman whip? When you fall under the weight of the cross, which disciple will be close enough to spring to your side and carry your burden?

None of them will.

But the cleansing is not just a gesture; it is a necessity. Listen to what Jesus said: "If I don't wash your feet, you are not one of my people" (John 13:8 NCV).

We will never be cleansed until we confess we are dirty. And we will never be able to wash the feet of those who have hurt us until we allow Jesus, the one we have hurt, to wash ours.

DAY 26

GO FIRST TO GOD

"Do not let your hearts be troubled.
Trust in God; trust also in me."
—JOHN 14:1

It's the expression of Jesus that puzzles us. We've never seen his face like this.

Jesus smiling, yes.

Jesus weeping, absolutely.

Jesus stern, even that.

But Jesus anguished? Cheeks streaked with tears? Face flooded in sweat? Rivulets of blood dripping from his chin? You remember the night.

"Jesus . . . kneeled down and prayed, 'Father, if you are willing, take away this cup of suffering. But do what you want, not what I want.' . . . His sweat was like drops of blood falling to the ground" (Luke 22:41–44 NCV).

Jesus was more than anxious; he was afraid. How remarkable that Jesus felt such fear. But how kind that he told us about it. We tend to do the opposite. Gloss over our fears. Cover them up. Keep our sweaty palms in our pockets, our nausea and dry mouths a secret. Not so with Jesus. We see no mask of strength. But we do hear a request for strength.

"Father, if you are willing, take away this cup of suffering." The first one to hear his fear is his Father. He could have gone to his mother. He could have confided in his disciples. He could have assembled a prayer meeting. All would have been appropriate, but none was his priority.

How did Jesus endure the terror of the crucifixion? He went first to the Father with his fears. He modeled the words of Psalm 56:3: "When I am afraid, I put my trust in you" (NLT).

Do the same with yours. Don't avoid life's Gardens of Gethsemane. Enter them. Just don't enter them alone. And while there, be honest. Pounding the ground is permitted. Tears are allowed. And if you sweat blood, you won't be the first. Do what Jesus did; open your heart.

DAY 27

UNBELIEVABLE BETRAYAL

*"You will leave me all alone. Yet I am not alone,
for my Father is with me."*
—JOHN 16:32

On the night before his death, a veritable landfill of woes tumbled in on Jesus. Somewhere between the Gethsemane prayer and the mock trial is what has to be the darkest scene in the history of the human drama.

"With [Judas] were many people carrying swords and clubs who had been sent from the leading priests. . . . Then the people came and grabbed Jesus and arrested him" (Matt. 26:47, 50 NCV).

Judas arrived with an angry crowd. John is even more specific. The term he employs is the Greek word *speira*, or a "group of soldiers" (John 18:3 NCV). At minimum, *speira* depicts a group of two hundred soldiers.

Surely in a group this size there is one person who will defend Jesus. He came to the aid of so many. All those sermons. All those miracles. We wait for the one person who will declare, "Jesus is an innocent man!" But no one does. The people he came to save have turned against him.

We can almost forgive the crowd. Their contact with Jesus was too brief, too casual. Perhaps they didn't know better. But the disciples did. They knew better. They knew *him* better. But did they defend Jesus? Hardly. The most bitter pill Jesus had to swallow was the unbelievable betrayal by the disciples. "All of Jesus' followers left him and ran away" (Matt. 26:56 NCV).

From a human point of view, Jesus's world had collapsed. No help from the people, no loyalty from his friends. But that's not how Jesus saw it. He saw something else entirely. He wasn't oblivious to the circumstances; he just wasn't limited to them. Somehow he was able to see good in the bad, the purpose in the pain, and God's presence in the problem.

DAY 28

THE POINT OF THE CROWN

"The soldiers of the governor took Jesus into the
Praetorium. . . . And they stripped Him and put a
scarlet robe on Him. When they had twisted a
crown of thorns, they put it on His head."
—MATTHEW 27:27–29 (NKJV)

Throughout Scripture thorns symbolize, not sin, but the conse-
quence of sin (Gen. 3:17–18; Num. 33:55; Prov. 22:5). The
fruit of sin is thorns—spiny, prickly, cutting thorns.

I emphasize the "point" of the thorns to suggest a point you
may have never considered: If the fruit of sin is thorns, isn't the
thorny crown on Christ's brow a picture of the fruit of our sin
that pierced his heart?

What is the fruit of sin? Step into the briar patch of humanity
and feel a few thistles. Shame. Disgrace. Discouragement. Anxiety.
Haven't our hearts been caught in these brambles?

The heart of Jesus, however, had not. He had never been cut by the thorns of sin. What you and I face daily, he never knew. Anxiety? He never worried! Guilt? He was never guilty! Jesus never knew the fruits of sin . . . until he became sin for us.

And when he did, all the emotions of sin tumbled in on him like shadows in a forest. He felt anxious, guilty, and alone. Can't you hear the emotion in his prayer? "My God, my God, why have you rejected me?" (Matt. 27:46 NCV). These are not the words of a saint. This is the cry of a sinner.

And this prayer is one of the most remarkable parts of his coming. But I can think of something even greater. Want to know what it is? Want to know the coolest thing about the One who gave up the crown of heaven for a crown of thorns?

He did it for you. Just for you.

DAY 29

THE FIRST STEP TO THE CROSS

"For God did not send his Son
into the world to condemn the world,
but to save the world through him."
—JOHN 3:17

The most notorious road in the world is the Via Dolorosa, "the Way of Sorrows." According to tradition, it is the route Jesus took from Pilate's hall to Calvary. The path is marked by stations frequently used by Christians for their devotions. One station marks the passing of Pilate's verdict. Another, the appearance of Simon to carry the cross. Three stations commemorate the stumbles of Christ, another the words of Christ. There are fourteen stations in all, each one a reminder of the events of Christ's final journey.

Is the route accurate? Probably not. When Jerusalem was destroyed in A.D. 70 and again in A.D. 135, the streets of the city were destroyed. As a result, no one knows the exact route Christ followed that Friday.

But we do know where the path actually began.

The path began, not in the court of Pilate, but in the halls of heaven. Jesus began his journey when he left his home in search of us. Armed with nothing more than a passion to win your heart, he came looking. His desire was singular—to bring God's children home. The Bible has a word for this quest: *reconciliation.*

"God was in Christ reconciling the world to Himself" (2 Cor. 5:19 NKJV). The Greek word for *reconcile* means "to render something otherwise."[1] Reconciliation restitches the unraveled, reverses the rebellion, rekindles the cold passion.

Reconciliation touches the shoulder of the wayward and woos him homeward.

The path to the cross tells us exactly how far God will go to call us back.

DAY 30

HE SAW THE LIST

"Jesus . . . endured the cross,
scorning its shame, and sat down
at the right hand of the throne of God."
—HEBREWS 12:2

Come with me to the hill of Calvary. Watch as the soldiers shove the Carpenter to the ground and stretch his arms against the beams. One presses a knee against a forearm and a spike against a hand. Jesus turns his face toward the nail just as the soldier lifts the hammer to strike it.

Couldn't Jesus have stopped him? With a flex of the biceps, with a clench of the fist, he could have resisted. Is this not the same hand that stilled the sea? Summoned the dead?

But the fist doesn't clench . . . and the moment isn't aborted.

The mallet rings and the skin rips and the blood begins to drip, then rush. Then the questions follow. Why? Why didn't Jesus resist?

"Because he loved us," we reply. That is true, wonderfully true, but—forgive me—only partially true. There is more to his reason. He saw something that made him stay. As the soldier pressed his arm, Jesus rolled his head to the side, and with his cheek resting on the wood, he saw:

A mallet? Yes.

A nail? Yes.

The soldier's hand? Yes.

But he saw something else. Between his hand and the wood, there was a list. A long list. A list of our mistakes: our lusts and lies and greedy moments and prodigal years. A list of our sins.

The bad decisions from last year. The bad attitudes from last week. There, in broad daylight for all of heaven to see, was a list of your mistakes.

He saw the list! He knew the price of those sins was death. He knew the source of those sins was you, and since he couldn't bear the thought of eternity without you, he chose the nails.

Day 31

Disgraced

"The next day John saw Jesus coming toward him
and said, 'Look, the Lamb of God,
who takes away the sin of the world!'"
—John 1:29

Every aspect of the crucifixion was intended not only to hurt the victim but to shame him. Death on a cross was usually reserved for the most vile offenders: slaves, murderers, assassins, and the like. The condemned person was marched through the city streets, shouldering his crossbar and wearing a placard about his neck that named his crime. At the execution site he was stripped and mocked.

Crucifixion was so abhorrent that Cicero wrote, "Let the very name of the cross be far away, not only from the body of a Roman citizen, but even from his thoughts, his eyes, his ears."[2]

Jesus was not only shamed before people, he was shamed before heaven.

Since he bore the sin of the murderer and adulterer, he felt the shame of the murderer and adulterer. Though he never lied, he bore the disgrace of a liar. Though he never cheated, he felt the embarrassment of a cheater. Since he bore the sin of the world, he felt the collective shame of the world.

While on the cross, Jesus felt the indignity and disgrace of a criminal. No, he was not guilty. No, he had not committed a sin. And, no, he did not deserve to be sentenced. But you and I were, we had, and we did.

"He changed places with us" (Gal. 3:13 NCV).

DAY 32

CHRIST'S CLOTHING ON THE
CROSS

*"They divided his clothes among the four of them.
They also took his robe, but it was seamless, woven
in one piece from the top. So they said, 'Let's not
tear it but throw dice to see who gets it.'"*
—JOHN 19:23–24 (NLT)

It must have been Jesus's finest possession. Jewish tradition called for a mother to make such a robe and present it to her son as a departure gift when he left home. Had Mary done this for Jesus? We don't know. But we do know the tunic was without seam, woven from top to bottom. Why is this significant?

Scripture often describes our behavior as the clothes we wear. Peter urges us to be "clothed with humility" (1 Pet. 5:5 NKJV). David speaks of evil people who clothe themselves "with cursing"

(Ps. 109:18 NKJV). Garments can symbolize character, and like his garment, Jesus's character was uninterrupted perfection.

The character of Jesus was a seamless fabric woven from heaven to earth . . . from God's thoughts to Jesus's actions. From God's tears to Jesus's compassion. From God's word to Jesus's response. All one piece.

But when Christ was nailed to the cross, he took off his robe of seamless perfection and assumed a different wardrobe, the wardrobe of indignity.

The indignity of nakedness. Stripped before his own mother and loved ones. Shamed before his family.

The indignity of failure. For a few pain-filled hours, the religious leaders were the victors, and Christ appeared the loser. Shamed before his accusers.

Worst of all, he wore *the indignity of sin.* "He himself bore our sins in his body on the tree" (1 Pet. 2:24).

The clothing of Christ on the cross? Sin—yours and mine. The sins of all humanity.

DAY 33

TWO THIEVES—TWO CHOICES

*"Therefore, there is now no condemnation
for those who are in Christ Jesus."*
—ROMANS 8:1

Ever wonder why there were two crosses next to Christ? Why not six or ten? Ever wonder why Jesus was in the center? Why not on the far right or far left? Could it be that the two crosses on the hill symbolize one of God's greatest gifts? The gift of choice.

The two criminals have so much in common. Convicted by the same system. Condemned to the same death. Surrounded by the same crowd. Equally close to the same Jesus. In fact, they begin with the same sarcasm: "The two criminals also said cruel things to Jesus" (Matt. 27:44 CEV).

But one changed. "He said, 'Jesus, remember me when you come into your kingdom.' Jesus said to him, 'I tell you the truth, today you will be with me in paradise'" (Luke 23:42–43 NCV).

Think about the thief who repented. Though we know little about him, we know this: He made some bad mistakes in life. He chose the wrong crowd, the wrong morals, the wrong behavior. But would you consider his life a waste? Is he spending eternity reaping the fruit of all the bad choices he made? No, just the opposite. He is enjoying the fruit of the one good choice he made. In the end all his bad choices were redeemed by a solitary good one.

You've made some bad choices in life, haven't you? You look back over your life and say, "If only . . . if only I could make up for those bad choices." You can. One good choice for eternity offsets a thousand bad ones on earth.

The choice is yours.

DAY 34

❧ ❧

ABANDONED BY GOD

"Surely he took up our infirmities and carried our
sorrows, yet we considered him stricken
by God, smitten by him, and afflicted."
—ISAIAH 53:4

Noises intermingle on the hill: Pharisees mocking, swords clang-
ing, and dying men groaning. Jesus scarcely speaks. When he
does, diamonds sparkle against velvet. He gives his killers grace
and his mother a son. He answers the prayer of a thief and asks
for a drink from a soldier.

Then, at midday, darkness falls like a curtain. "At noon the
whole country was covered with darkness, which lasted for three
hours" (Matt. 27:45 TEV).

This is a supernatural darkness. Not a casual gathering of
clouds or a brief eclipse of the sun. This is a three-hour blanket

of blackness. Merchants in Jerusalem light candles. Soldiers ignite torches. The universe grieves. The sky weeps.

Christ lifts his heavy head and eyelids toward the heavens and spends his final energy crying out toward the ducking stars. "'*Eli, Eli, lema sabachthani?*' which means, 'My God, my God, why did you abandon me?'" (v. 46 TEV).

We would ask the same. Why him? Why forsake your Son? Forsake the murderers. Desert the evildoers. Turn your back on perverts and peddlers of pain. Abandon them, not him. Why would you abandon earth's only sinless soul?

What did Christ feel on the cross? The icy displeasure of a sin-hating God. Why? Because he "carried our sins in his body" (1 Pet. 2:24 NCV).

With hands nailed open, he invited God, "Treat me as you would treat them!" And God did. In an act that broke the heart of the Father, yet honored the holiness of heaven, sin-purging judgment flowed over the sinless Son of the ages.

And heaven gave earth her finest gift: the Lamb of God who took away the sin of the world.

"My God, my God, why did you abandon me?" Why did Christ scream those words? So you'll never have to.

DAY 35

"It Is Finished"

*"Looking unto Jesus, the author
and finisher of our faith."*
—HEBREWS 12:2 (NKJV)

The face of Jesus softened, and an afternoon dawn broke as he spoke a final time. "It is finished. . . . Father, into your hands I commit my spirit" (John 19:30; Luke 23:46).

As he gave his final breath, the earth gave a sudden stir. A rock rolled, and a soldier stumbled. Then, as suddenly as the silence was broken, the silence returned.

And now all is quiet. The mocking has ceased. There is no one to mock.

The soldiers are busy with the business of cleaning up the dead. Two men have come. Dressed well and meaning well, they are given the body of Jesus.

And we are left with the relics of his death. Three nails in a bin. Three cross-shaped shadows. A braided crown with scarlet tips.

Bizarre, isn't it? The thought that this blood is not man's blood but God's?

Crazy, isn't it? To think that these nails held your sins to a cross?

Absurd, don't you agree? That a scoundrel's prayer was offered and answered? Or more absurd that another scoundrel offered no prayer at all?

Absurdities and ironies. The hill of Calvary is nothing if not both.

We would have scripted the moment differently. Ask us how a God should redeem his world, and we will show you! White horses, flashing swords. Evil flat on his back. God on his throne.

But God on a cross? A split-lipped, puffy-eyed, blood-masked God on a cross? Sponge thrust in his face? Spear plunged in his side? Dice tossed at his feet?

No, we wouldn't have written the drama of redemption this way. But, then again, we weren't asked to. These players and props were heaven picked and God ordained. We were not asked to design the hour.

But we have been asked to respond to it.

Day 36

Secret Friends

"Going to Pilate, [Joseph] asked for Jesus' body,
and Pilate ordered that it be given to him."
—Matthew 27:58

They are coming as friends—secret friends—but friends nonetheless. "You can take him down now, soldier. I'll take care of him."

A soldier leans a ladder against the center tree, ascends it, and removes the stake that holds the beam to the upright part of the cross. Two of the other soldiers, glad that the day's work is nearing completion, assist with the heavy chore of laying the cypress crosspiece and body on the ground.

"Careful now," says Joseph.

The five-inch nails are wrenched from the hard wood. The body that encased a Savior is lifted and laid on a large rock.

"He's yours," says the sentry.

The two are not accustomed to this type of work. Yet their hands move quickly to their tasks.

Joseph of Arimathea kneels behind the head of Jesus and tenderly wipes the wounded face. With a soft, wet cloth he cleans the blood that came in the garden, that came from the lashings and from the crown of thorns. With this done, he closes the eyes tight.

Nicodemus unrolls some linen sheeting that Joseph brought and places it on the rock beside the body. The two Jewish leaders lift the lifeless body of Jesus and set it on the linen. Parts of the body are now anointed with perfumed spices. As Nicodemus touches the cheeks of the Master with aloe, the emotion he has been containing escapes. His own tear falls on the face of the crucified King. He pauses to brush away another. The middle-aged Jew looks longingly at the young Galilean.

The high society of Jerusalem wasn't going to look too kindly on two of their religious leaders burying a revolutionist. But for Joseph and Nicodemus the choice was obvious. And, besides, they'd much rather save their souls than their skin.

DAY 37

IT'S ALL RIGHT TO DREAM AGAIN

"As the new day was dawning . . ."
—MATTHEW 28:1 (NLT)

Mary, the mother of James, and Mary Magdalene have come to the tomb to place warm oils on a cold body and bid farewell to the one man who gave reason to their hopes.

The women think they are alone. They aren't. They think their journey is unnoticed. They are wrong. God knows. And he has a surprise waiting for them.

"An angel of the Lord came down from heaven, went to the tomb, and rolled the stone away from the entrance" (Matt. 28:2 NCV).

Why did the angel move the stone? For whom did he roll away the rock?

For Jesus? That's what I always thought. But think about it. Did the stone have to be removed in order for Jesus to exit? Did God have to have help? Was the death conqueror so weak that he couldn't push away a rock?

I don't think so. The text gives the impression that Jesus was already out when the stone was moved! For whom, then, was the stone moved?

Listen to what the angel says: "Come and see the place where his body was" (v. 6 NCV).

The stone was moved—not for Jesus—but for the women; not so Jesus could come out, but so the women could see in!

Mary looks at Mary Magdalene, and Mary is grinning the same grin she had when the bread and fish kept coming out of the basket. Suddenly it's all right to dream again.

"Go quickly and tell his followers, 'Jesus has risen from the dead. He is going into Galilee ahead of you, and you will see him there,'" the angel says (v. 7 NCV).

Mary and Mary don't have to be told twice. They turn and start running to Jerusalem. The darkness is gone. The sun is up. The Son is out.

DAY 38

VICTORY RAGS

*"Every detail in our lives of love for
God is worked into something good."*
—ROMANS 8:28 (MSG)

Very early on Sunday morning Peter and John were given the news: "Jesus's body is missing!" Instantly the two disciples hurried to the sepulcher, John outrunning Peter and arriving first. What he saw so stunned him he froze at the entrance.

What did he see? "Strips of linen cloth." He saw "the cloth that had been around Jesus' head . . . folded up and laid in a different place from the strips of linen." He saw "cloth lying" (John 20:5–7 NCV).

The original Greek provides helpful insight here. John employs a term that means "rolled up," "still in their folds." These burial wraps had not been ripped off and thrown down.

They were still in their original state! The linens were undisturbed. The graveclothes were still rolled and folded.

How could this be?

If friends had removed the body, would they not have taken the clothes with it? If foes had taken the body, would they not have done the same?

If not, if for some reason friends or foes had unwrapped the body, would they have been so careful as to dispose of the clothing in such an orderly fashion? Of course not!

But if neither friend nor foe took the body, who did?

This was John's question, and this question led to John's discovery. "He saw and believed" (v. 8 NCV).

Through the rags of death, John saw the power of life. Odd, don't you think, that God would use something as sad as a burial wrap to change a life?

But God is given to such practices:

In his hand, empty wine jugs at a wedding become a symbol of power.

A crude manger in Bethlehem is his symbol of devotion.

And a tool of death is a symbol of his love.

DAY 39

GRACE BEFORE BREAKFAST

"'Now come and have some breakfast!'
Jesus said."
—JOHN 21:12 (NLT)

Peter's thoughts are interrupted by a shout from the shore. "Catch any fish?"

Peter and John look up. Probably a villager. "No!" they yell.

"Try the other side!" the voice yells back.

John looks at Peter. What harm? So out sails the net. Peter wraps the rope around his wrist to wait.

But there is no wait. The rope pulls taut, and the net catches. Peter sets his weight against the side of the boat and begins to bring in the net. He's so intense with the task, he misses the message.

John doesn't. The moment is déjà vu. This has happened before. The long night. The empty net. The call to cast again.

211

Fish flapping on the floor of the boat. Wait a minute . . . He lifts his eyes to the man on the shore. "It's him," he whispers.

Then louder, "It's Jesus."

Peter turns and looks. Jesus, the God of heaven and earth, is on the shore . . . and he's building a fire.

Peter plunges into the water, swims to the shore, and stumbles out wet and shivering and stands in front of the friend he betrayed. Jesus has prepared a bed of coals.

For one of the few times in his life, Peter is silent. What words would suffice? The moment is too holy for words. God is offering breakfast to the friend who betrayed him. And Peter is once again finding grace at Galilee.

DAY 40

HIS LIFE MEANS LIFE

"My purpose is to give life."
—JOHN 10:10 (NLT)

The heart of Jesus was pure. The Savior was adored by thousands, yet content to live a simple life. He was cared for by women (Luke 8:1–3), yet never accused of lustful thoughts; scorned by his own creation, but willing to forgive them before they even requested his mercy. Peter, who traveled with Jesus for three and a half years, described him as a "lamb unblemished and spotless" (1 Pet. 1:19 NASB). After spending the same amount of time with Jesus, John concluded, "And in him is no sin" (1 John 3:5).

Jesus's heart was peaceful. The disciples fretted over the need to feed the thousands, but not Jesus. He thanked God for the problem. The disciples shouted for fear in the storm, but not Jesus. He slept through it. Peter drew his sword to fight the soldiers, but not Jesus. He lifted his hand to heal. His heart was at peace. When his disciples abandoned him, did he pout and go home? When Peter denied him, did Jesus lose his temper? When the soldiers spit in his face, did he breathe fire in theirs? Far from it. He was at peace. He forgave them. He refused to be guided by vengeance.

He also refused to be guided by anything other than his high call. His heart was purposeful. Most lives aim at nothing in particular and achieve it. Jesus aimed at one goal—to save humanity from its sin. He could summarize his life with one sentence: "The Son of man came to seek and to save the lost" (Luke 19:10 RSV).

The same one who saved your soul longs to remake your heart. God is willing to change us into the likeness of the Savior. Shall we accept his offer?

NOTES

CHAPTER 1: THE MOST FAMOUS CONVERSATION IN THE BIBLE

1. A colonnade on the east of the temple, so called from a tradition that it was a relic of Solomon's temple left standing after the destruction of Jerusalem by the Babylonians. (See *Bible Encyclopedia*, "Solomon's Porch," ChristianAnswers.net, http://www.christiananswers.net/dictionary/porchsolomons.html.)

2. The earliest copies of the books of the New Testament were written in Greek, so Greek word studies shed light on the meaning of New Testament passages.

3. *The New Testament Greek Lexicon*, "pa/lin," Heartlight's SearchGodsWord, http://www.searchgodsword.org/lex/grk/browse.cgi?letter=p&sn=21&pn=2.

4. Ibid., "anothen," Heartlight's SearchGodsWord, http://www.searchgodsword.org/lex/grk/view.cgi?number=509&1=en.

5. Stanley Barnes, comp., *Sermons on John 3:16* (Greenville, SC: Ambassador Productions, 1999), 90.

6. James Montgomery Boice, *The Gospel of John: An Expositional Commentary* (Grand Rapids: Zondervan Publishing House, 1985), 195.

7. Barnes, *Sermons on John 3:16*, 25.

CHAPTER 2: NO ONE LIKE HIM

1. Andy Christofides, *The Life Sentence: John 3:16* (Waynesboro, GA: Paternoster Publishing, 2002), 11.

2. Guillermo Gonzalez and Jay W. Richards, *The Privileged Planet: How Our Place in the Cosmos Is Designed for Discovery* (Washington, DC: Regnery Publishing, 2004), 143.

3. Christofides, *The Life Sentence*, 13.

4. "Liftoff to Space Exploration," NASA, http://liftoff.msfc.nasa.gov/academy/universe_travel.html.

5. Bob Sheehan, "A Self-Revealing God," *Reformation Today,* no. 127, May–June 1992, 6.
6. Carl Sagan, *Pale Blue Dot: A Vision of the Human Future in Space* (New York: Ballantine Books, 1994), 7, quoted in Gonzalez and Richards, *The Privileged Planet,* x.
7. Bill Tucker (speech, Oak Hills Church men's conference, San Antonio, TX, May 3, 2003).

CHAPTER 3: HOPE FOR THE HARD HEART
1. Thomas Maeder, "A Few Hundred People Turned to Bone," *Atlantic Online,* http://www.theatlantic.com/doc/199802/bone.

CHAPTER 4: WHEN YOU GET BOOTED OUT
1. Ker Than, "Pluto Is Now Just a Number: 134340," MSNBC.com, http://msnbc.msn.com/id/14789691.
2. John S. Feinberg, gen. ed., *No One Like Him: The Doctrine of God* (Wheaton, IL: Crossway Books, 2001), 349.
3. R. Laird Harris, Gleason Archer, and Bruce K. Waltke, eds. *Theological Wordbook of the Old Testament,* vol. 1 (Chicago: Moody, 1980), 332, quoted in Feinberg, *No One Like Him,* 349.
4. Ernest K. Emurian, *Living Stories of Famous Hymns* (Boston: W. A. Wilde Company, 1955), 99–100, and Robert J. Morgan, *Then Sings My Soul: 150 of the World's Greatest Hymn Stories* (Nashville: Thomas Nelson, 2003), 207.
5. W. E. Vine, *Expository Dictionary of New Testament Words: A Comprehensive Dictionary of the Original Greek Words with Their Precise Meanings for English Readers* (McClean: VA: MacDonald Publishing Company, n.d.), 703.
6. Tim Russert, *Wisdom of Our Fathers: Lessons and Letters from Daughters and Sons* (New York: Random House, 2006), 235–36.

CHAPTER 5: THE ONLY ONE AND ONLY
1. James R. White, *The Forgotten Trinity: Recovering the Heart of Christian Belief* (Minneapolis: Bethany House Publishers, 1998), 201–3, note 27.
2. Edward W. Goodrick, ed., John R. Kohlenberger III and James A. Swann, assoc. eds., *Zondervan NIV Exhaustive Concordance,* 2nd ed. (Grand Rapids, MI: Zondervan Publishing House, 1999), 4778, #4742.

CHAPTER 6: THE HEART HE OFFERS
1. The Hunger Site, http://www.thehungersite.com.
2. Os Guinness, *Unspeakable: Facing Up to Evil in an Age of Genocide and Terror* (San Francisco: HarperSanFrancisco, 2005), 4–5.

3. Edward W. Goodrick, ed., John R. Kohlenberger III and James A. Swann, assoc. eds., *Zondervan NIV Exhaustive Concordance, 2nd ed.* (Grand Rapids, MI: Zondervan Publishing House, 1999), 4778, #4742.
4. Stanley Barnes, comp., *Sermons on John 3:16* (Greenville, SC: Ambassador Productions, 1999), 79.
5. Donald Grey Barnhouse, *Let Me Illustrate: More Than 400 Stories, Anecdotes & Illustrations* (Grand Rapids: Fleming H. Revell, 1967), 196.
6. Adapted from Steven Vryhof, "Crash Helmets and Church Bells," *Perspectives,* August-September 2000, 3, quoted in Leanne Van Dyk, *Believing in Jesus Christ* (Louisville, KY: Geneva Press, 2002), 109–10.

CHAPTER 7: HEAVEN'S "WHOEVER" POLICY
1. Francis William Boreham, *A Handful Of Stars,* quoted in Barnes, comp., *Sermons on John 3:16* (Greenville, SC: Ambassador Productions, 1999), 19–20. The wording of the verse probably followed the most popular English translation of the day, the King James Version: "For God so loved the world, that he gave his only begotten Son, that whosoever believeth in him should not perish, but have everlasting life."
2. Larry Dixon, *The Other Side of the Good News* (Wheaton, IL: Victor Books, 1992), 133.

CHAPTER 9: GOD'S GRACIOUS GRIP
1. David Tereshchuk, "Racing Towards Inclusion," Team Hoyt, http://www.teamhoyt.com/history.shtml.
2. R. C. Zaehner, ed., *Encyclopedia of World Religions* (New York: Barnes & Noble, 1997), s.v. "Hinduism."
3. Dan McKinley, "Aren't All Religions Just Different Ways to the Same Place?" The Coaching Center, http://www.gocampus.org/modx/index.php?id=109.
4. John Blanchard, *Whatever Happened to Hell?* (Wheaton, IL: Crossway Books, 1995), 62.
5. Dave Hunt, *Whatever Happened to Heaven?* (Eugene, OR: Harvest House Publishers, 1988), 14, quoted in Blanchard, *Whatever Happened to Hell?* 62.
6. Peter Cotterell, *London Bible College Review,* Summer 1989, quoted in Peter Lewis, *The Glory of Christ* (London: Hodder and Stoughton, 1992), 461.
7. Michael Green, *You Must Be Joking: Popular Excuses for Avoiding Jesus Christ* (London: Hodder and Stoughton, 1981), 43, quoted in Lewis, *The Glory of Christ,* 461.
8. Green, *You Must Be Joking,* 43, quoted in Lewis, *The Glory of Christ,* 461.

CHAPTER 10: HELL'S SUPREME SURPRISE

1. 1 Cor. 1:18.
2. Robert Jeffress, *Hell? Yes! . . . and Other Outrageous Truths You Can Still Believe* (Colorado Springs, CO: WaterBrook Press, 2004), 71–72.
3. Martin Marty, *Newsweek,* March 27, 1989, quoted in Blanchard, *Whatever Happened to Hell?*, 15–16.
4. Jeffress, *Hell? Yes!*, 73.
5. Blanchard, *Whatever Happened to Hell?*, 105.
6. Vine, *Expository Dictionary of New Testament Words*, 867.
7. James Denney, *Studies in Theology* (London: Hodder and Stoughton, 1904), 255, quoted in Bruce Demarest, *The Cross and Salvation: The Doctrine of Salvation* (Wheaton, IL: Crossway Books, 1997), 31.
8. Thomas Vincent, *Christ's Certain and Sudden Appearance to Judgment,* quoted in Eryl Davies, *The Wrath of God,* (Evangelical Press of Wales), 50, quoted in Blanchard, *Whatever Happened to Hell?*, 145.
9. C. S. Lewis, *The Problem of Pain* (New York: MacMillan, 1962), 127, quoted in Blanchard, *Whatever Happened to Hell?*, 152.

CHAPTER 11: WHAT MAKES HEAVEN HEAVENLY

1. Randy Alcorn, *Heaven* (Wheaton, IL: Tyndale House Publishers, 2004), 6–7.
2. Ibid., 393.
3. Robert Strand, *Moments for Mothers* (Green Forest, AR: New Leaf Press, 1996), excerpted in Jack Canfield and others, *A 4th Course of Chicken Soup for the Soul: 101 More Stories to Open the Heart and Rekindle the Spirit* (Deerfield Beach, FL: Health Communications, 1997), 200–01.

CHAPTER 12: THE LAST WORD ON LIFE

1. Vine, *Expository Dictionary of New Testament Words*, 676.
2. Blanchard, *Whatever Happened to Hell?*, 54.
3. Eph. 2:1.
4. Eph. 4:18.
5. 1 John 5:1 NKJV.
6. John 1:13 NLT.

CONCLUSION

1. Acts 26:20; Rom. 10:9; Acts 2:38.

40 DAYS OF DEVOTIONS

1. Frank Stagg, *New Testament Theology* (Nashville: Broadman Press, 1962), 102.
2. Josef Blinzler, *The Trial of Jesus: The Jewish and Roman Proceedings Against Jesus Christ Described and Assessed from the Oldest Accounts,* trans., Isabel McHugh and Florence McHugh (Westminster, MD: The Newman Press, 1959), 103.

BIBLIOGRAPHY FOR 40 DAYS OF DEVOTIONS

The Applause of Heaven (Dallas: Word, 1990).

Cure for the Common Life: Living in Your Sweet Spot (Nashville: W Publishing Group, 2005).

A Gentle Thunder: Hearing God Through the Storm (Dallas: Word, 1995).

God Came Near (Portland: Multnomah, 1987).

The Great House of God: A Home for Your Heart (Dallas: Word, 1997).

He Chose the Nails: What God Did to Win Your Heart (Nashville: Word, 2000).

He Still Moves Stones (Dallas: Word, 1993).

Just Like Jesus (Nashville: Word, 1998).

A Love Worth Giving: Living in the Overflow of God's Love (Nashville: W Publishing Group, 2002).

Next Door Savior (Nashville: W Publishing Group, 2003).

No Wonder They Call Him the Savior (Portland: Multnomah, 1986).

Traveling Light: Releasing the Burdens You Were Never Intended to Bear (Nashville: W Publishing Group, 2001).

When God Whispers Your Name (Dallas: Word, 1994).

Hope. Pure and simple.

The Teaching Ministry of Max Lucado

You're invited to partner with UpWords to bring radio and the Internet a message of hope, pure and simple, in Jesus Christ!

Visit www.maxlucado.com to find FREE valuable resources for spiritual growth and encouragement, such as:

- Archives of UpWords, Max's daily radio program. You will also find a listing of radio stations and broadcast times in your area.
- Daily devotionals
- Book excerpts
- Exclusive features and presentations
- Subscription information on how you can receive email messages from Max
- Downloads of audio, video, and printed material

You will also find an online store and special offers.

Call toll-free,
1-800-822-9673

for more information and to order by phone.

UpWords Ministries
P.O. Box 692170
San Antonio, TX 78269-2170
1-800-822-9673
www.maxlucado.com

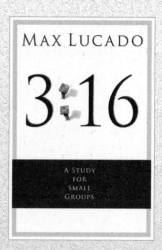

If 9/11 are the numbers of terror and despair, then 3:16 are the numbers of hope. Best-selling author Max Lucado leads readers through a word-by-word study of John 3:16, the passage that he calls the "Hope Diamond" of scripture. The study includes 12 lessons that are designed to work with both the trade book and the Indelible DVD for a multi-media experience.

Listen to the message of 3:16 in your home or take it on the road. This CD makes the perfect gift for the family or friends you want to hear the hope found in John 3:16.

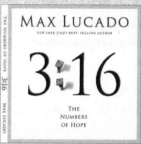

3:16 is also available in Spanish, Portuguese, German, Swedish, Dutch, Korean, Japanese, and Chinese.

GOD'S GREAT BIG LOVE FOR ME

With colored beads built right in, this board book is the perfect book to teach the verse and meaning behind John 3:16 to preschool children.
Available February 2008

3:16 – THE NUMBERS OF HOPE TEEN EDITION

Max offers his unique and simple storytelling for this important message while Tricia Goyer writes teen responses to Max's message, guiding teens to fully understand how this verse can impact their lives. From confession to praise, these responses are sure to bring an insightful look into the personal faith of teens.
Available February 2008

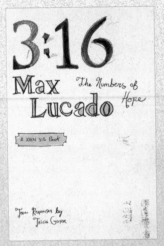

A DVD FOR SMALL GROUP STUDY

This is a kit designed and priced specifically for small groups. It will include a copy of the study guide for small groups, an evangelism booklet, the Indelible DVD, and a CD-ROM with facilitator's guide information and promotional material.

3:16 SONGS OF HOPE CD

Featuring songs and artists inspired by the book *3:16*. The two disc set will also include DVD-Rom featuring digital Bible study material.

3:16 STORIES OF HOPE DVD

This DVD product will feature 12 compelling moments of hope with Max Lucado. It will include a short, evangelistic film conveying through drama and metaphor the 3:16 promise. It will also provide musical elements and interviews with artists.

Share the message of *3:16* with t-shirts and ball caps.

A complementary jewelry line will be available from Bob Siemon Designs.

ONE

THE CAMPAIGN TO MAKE
POVERTY HISTORY
WWW.ONE.ORG

There is a plague of biblical proportions taking place in Africa right now, but we can beat this crisis, if we each do our part. Step ONE is signing the ONE petition, to join the ONE Campaign.

The ONE Campaign is a new effort to rally Americans—ONE by ONE—to fight global AIDS and extreme poverty. We are engaging Americans everywhere we gather—in churches and synagogues, on the internet and college campuses, at community meetings and concerts. To learn more about The ONE Campaign, go to www.one.org and sign the online petition.

> "Use your uniqueness to take great risks for God! If you're great with kids, volunteer at the orphanage. If you have a head for business, start a soup kitchen. If God bent you toward medicine, dedicate a day or a decade to AIDS patients. The only mistake is not to risk making one."
>
> —Max Lucado, *Cure for the Common Life*

ONE Voice can make a difference.
Let God work through you; join the ONE Campaign now!

This campaign is brought to you by